The Unmoored God

The Unmoored God

Believing in a Time of Dislocation

Paul G. Crowley, SJ

Founded in 1970, Orbis Books endeavors to publish works that enlighten the mind, nourish the spirit, and challenge the conscience. The publishing arm of the Maryknoll Fathers and Brothers, Orbis seeks to explore the global dimensions of the Christian faith and mission, to invite dialogue with diverse cultures and religious traditions, and to serve the cause of reconciliation and peace. The books published reflect the views of their authors and do not represent the official position of the Maryknoll Society. To learn more about Maryknoll and Orbis Books, please visit our website at www.maryknollsociety.org.

Published by Orbis Books, Box 302, Maryknoll, NY 10545-0302.

Manufactured in the United States of America

Library of Congress Cataloging-in-Publication Data

Names: Crowley, Paul G., author.
Title: The unmoored God : believing in a time of dislocation / Paul G. Crowley.
Description: Maryknoll : Orbis Books, 2017. | Includes bibliographical references and index.
Identifiers: LCCN 2017022185 | ISBN 9781626982468 (pbk.)
Subjects: LCSH: Faith | God (Christianity) | Christianity and culture. | Catholic Church—Doctrines.
Classification: LCC BV4637.C759 2017 | DDC 234/.23—dc23 LC record available at hhtps://lccn.loc.giv/2017022185

If you are called Love I adore only you, Lord,
If you are called Goodness I adore only you,
If you are called Pardon I adore only you, Lord,
If you are called Passion, I adore only you.
My prayer rises to you who are so far from me now,
To you who are so far.
Forgive me for having doubted your love,
Forgive me for having doubted you!
You who gave your life for me,
Forgive me for having remained so distant.
Now that it is you who are distant,
Are you still there to hear my prayers?
Now it is you who are distant,
Now you are the distant love, Lord,
Lord, you are love,
You are the distant love . . .

—Amin Maalouf
"Love from Afar"

For

Denise Lardner Carmody

and

Michael J. Buckley, SJ

Mentors and Friends

Contents

Preface ix

Introduction: God Unmoored 1

1. The Problem of Believing in a Dislocated God 19
2. Homelessness in the Face of Suffering 38
3. The Dislocation of the Divine Kenosis 51
4. The Dislocation of Solidarity with the Crucified 61
5. The Dislocation of Discipleship 74

Epilogue: Toward a Mystagogy of Believing 89

Bibliography 97

Notes 107

Index 127

Preface

As I put the finishing touches on this book, the country of which I am a citizen has, through a single election, decided to change course in what seems like a 180-degree turn. The implications of this vote for the world at large are potentially momentous. On the day after the election, I turned to the writings of Dietrich Bonhoeffer, and wondered whether we were set upon a "Bonhoeffer moment," as one Twitter tweet put it—a time when what it meant to believe, to hold true to Christian faith, would come at great cost. The shock of that morning was, in a certain sense, a clarion call to come to grips yet again with what it means to be a Christian, to believe in the person and message of Jesus, in a time of such dramatic political dislocation. So a time of darkness may prove to be a true *kairos*, an opportunity to rediscover the depths of faith, the passion of entering into the act of believing.

For the political dislocations of the age are merely the tip of the iceberg, floating atop a hidden, subsurface motion of the human spirit. Some events can occur only when, it seems, that God seems no longer near—when God's relation to us, or our relation to God, is uncertain, and when God seems untethered from the earth, unmoored. The premise of this book is that existential and spiritual dislocation is occasioned by events of history which have upended the place of the human person in relation to God to such a degree that belief itself has been thrown up in the air. Of course, we do not notice most of this, for the machinery of ordinary religion rolls on, and all of this upheaval is papered over in religious bromides and what Karl Rahner called the "analgesic" of religion (and what Marx called the opiate of the people). Perhaps we are not living in a Bonhoeffer moment so much as a Nietzschean moment, when the madman in the marketplace turns out to be the only one who really comprehends what is going on. It is that madman to whom we should be listening in our time, for maybe, if we do, we might rediscover the God from whom we have turned away and realize that God has been unmoored by our own doing.

The gift of the time of historic turning is that it can force us into that political mysticism so eloquently described by Johannes Metz, a political mysticism that leads us to gaze into the transcendent depths of the human person, as described by his teacher, Karl Rahner. Rahner was a Jesuit, himself influenced by the Trinitarian and apostolic mysticism of Saint Ignatius, among other spiritual forebears. And in the faith imagination of Ignatius, God, newly unmoored in Ignatius's age by the fissures of the Reformation, as well as by the implications of a new cosmology, was nevertheless near. For Ignatius would bring God back to earth, not through a theological sleight of hand, but through a reformulation of how God is present: how divine Providence works on our behalf, raining grace down on believer and unbeliever alike. And although this grace has the power to crush us, like a thunderous waterfall, it in fact would enter into the human soul, and into human history, very subtly, like water falling on a sponge. And thus, from the depths of the human spirit, would human beings discover again what believing means—what it feels like. And it feels like rediscovering the disruptive power of the Gospel not in strength, but in weakness, and in following in the pathways of Jesus.

Believing is not simply an intellectual achievement; it is an existential act in response to a divine initiative. Dislocated humanity is met by a God who chooses a divine dislocation in the Incarnation, entering simply and intimately into our own human condition and showing the way, through suffering, toward life. Believing in *this* unmoored God would require entering into solidarity with unmoored humanity, and journeying with those who suffer, just as God did in Jesus. In this small book I propose to enter into an extended essay on this understanding of believing in God.

* * *

Thanks go to my colleagues Frederick Parrella, who helped me track down a reference in the sermons of Paul Tillich, and Ana Maria Pineda, RSM, who helped me track down a sermon by Archbishop Oscar Romero, and to research assistants Jonathan Homrighausen and Isaiah Green. I also wish to express my gratitude to Robert Ellsberg, publisher at Orbis Books, for his uncommon patience, and to Maria Angelini, production manager at Orbis.

Finally, I offer my great thanks to John D. Murphy, SJ, of Loyola University Chicago for reading through the manuscript and entering into very helpful dialogue with me about it. My friendship with John goes back many years, and I am deeply in his debt for so much.

This book is dedicated to two mentors and friends, Denise Carmody, provost emerita of Santa Clara, and Michael J. Buckley, SJ, Augustin Cardinal Bea Professor Emeritus of Theology at Santa Clara.

Without Denise's encouragement, this book would not have been finished. Denise has been my central mentor in the ways of academe and a friend since my undergraduate days at Stanford. There, she and her late husband John, then a graduate student, took me under their wings and introduced me to the joys of writing and also to the work of Rahner. I am grateful to her, not least because she has shown me by her example how to open myself wisely to God's promptings, even when I might not see them.

Michael Buckley was my earliest mentor in the Ignatian way and later, when I worked as his first research assistant, in the realms of serious scholarship. Through the years our companionship blossomed into a friendship that I deeply treasure. I shall ever be grateful to him for the many ways he has helped me and a whole generation of his students at Berkeley, Notre Dame, and Boston College, to aspire to his sublime blend of theological learning, spiritual wisdom, and generosity of spirit.

Both these mentors, also friends, are testament to what Simone Weil meant when she wrote to Father Perrin:

The greatest blessing you have brought me is of another order. In gaining my friendship by your charity (which I have never met anything to equal), you have provided me with a source of the most compelling and pure inspiration that is to be found among human things. For nothing among human things has such power to keep our gaze fixed ever more intensely upon God, than friendship for the friends of God.

Santa Clara, California
July 31, 2017
Feast of St. Ignatius Loyola

Introduction: God Unmoored

Oh, in childhood, God, how easy you were:
you, whom I cannot take hold of now, anywhere.
—Rainer Maria Rilke
"Oh, in Childhood," in *The Unknown Rilke*

For many people, believing in God is more difficult today than it might have been in the past. There are personal reasons, some of which Rilke alludes to: the passage of the years that bring in their wake so much suffering, wonderment about the meaning of faith, and one's own impatience with the God that a weakened church has given to people as the God of faith. Rilke is speaking of the loss of the God who made sense in a more innocent age.

But there are other reasons why believing in God has become problematic. Most of us live in a world of religious diversity and multiple overlapping belongings and identities, one where certainties have given way to cascades of open questions, one evolving from another. There is now a cultural atmosphere, at least in the global North, for seriously asking what truth, much less "the" truth, really is.

Another part of the problem for believing lies in the fact that the old world in which believing took root and grew and developed into religious practices and institutions has gradually evaporated. That former world is a world lost to many contemporary people. Along with the disappearance of that world has come the dislocation of God from the picture that once had a place for him: God has become unmoored from his bearings. It must be added that much of that former world was marked by what some came to see as a flimsy architecture of faith, or one indistinguishable from a dense and insulated culture interlaced with the church as an institution. Still, for many, God has not only become unmoored, but lost, only to be replaced by various forms of secular humanism, pious agnosticism, spiritual fads, and atheism.

The premise of this book is that believing can be creatively rediscovered through the experience of dislocation—our own and God's. Further, this rediscovery will coincide with reimagining God in relation to ourselves, not as easily located, the way he once was in the "childhood" of modernity, but precisely as dislocated, unmoored. The claim here will be that dislocation belongs to the very nature of the God who reveals himself to Israel and, ultimately, in Jesus, as the dislocated incarnation of this God, but also as the outpouring of this God as love, even through the ultimate dislocation of death by crucifixion. This reimagining of God tells what it means to believe, not by focusing on truths that can be located or mapped within a clear geography of religion but by focusing on the dislocation of believers themselves, wanderers that we are in the chaos of creation, longing for the place where we can find God. Believers are then pilgrims, like Jesus, who had no place to lay his head, no place finally to call home.

What do I mean by "dislocation"? Although this notion will be explored in various ways and from different angles in the pages that follow, a preliminary sketch might prove helpful here. First, I am speaking of the dislocations that could be said to describe the *human* situation as we know it. In the Christian theological tradition, the fundamental dislocation is captured by the myth of the Fall, the rupture between humankind and God represented by the "original sin" of the first parents of the human race. Genesis 3 is describing an *ontological* disjointedness that drives to the heart of what it means to be a human being: an alienation of human beings not only from God, who confirms the breach with his judgment upon Adam and Eve, but of human beings from themselves, ushering a realm and subsequent history of sin into human experience. This history of sin, in turn, leads to an experience of death and of suffering as marks of evil insinuating itself into human existence. This ontological dislocation results in a set of *existential* dislocations—found at the level of temporal and historical experience—ranging from the aftermath of personal tragedies to great social ills that result from systemic injustice, oppression, and violence. The massive global phenomenon of migration is one of the obvious examples of existential dislocation. A third type of dislocation, *spiritual* dislocation, has been brought about by shifting patterns of life—from changing gender constructs, to realignment of institutional and political loyalties, to the development of new cosmologies and the search for intelligent life beyond planet Earth. We live in what Martin Buber called an "epoch of homelessness" (to be discussed later), and this provides the contemporary context for our experience of ontological and existential dislocation. It also results in a radical sense of disconnectedness from God as a presence and guarantor of coherence.

That is the human side of the equation. But there is also a *divine* side—a set of "divine dislocations" that also have to be taken into account. There is first the sense that the God of Abraham, Isaac, and Jacob is presented in the Scriptures as an elusive mystery: God is personal and dwells among God's people, and yet God is also elusive and not fixed to any one place. Altars get built, but they do not remain fixed; the Holy of Holies at first resides not in temple, but in a movable tent. The God of Israel is mobile, in sharp contrast with the fixity of other gods. But there is also the sense that this very same God goes out of the way to meet the chosen people in their own ontological and existential dislocations—by dislocating God's Self and entering into the chaos of their creaturely dislocations. In Jesus, this God of dislocation meets the human race precisely in its dislocation, specifically in the existential dislocation of Israel under Roman rule. The human race is given the hope of finding its way "home" in God, of finding that place that is no longer imaginary, but in fact a land, a place to dwell. And on the spiritual plane that place of dwelling, as Jesus disclosed, was to be a Reign of God's love, where all ontological and existential forms of dislocation would be superseded. But this would take place and be accomplished by his disciples, following Jesus in solidarity with those who suffer dislocation even now. This form of discipleship would divulge a way of believing through practicing the dislocation of following Jesus, of loving in the way God first loved us (1 Jn 4:19).

This book suggests that the fundamental underlying cause of a loss of belief in God is that God has become dislocated and is no longer a part of the world picture for many former or would-be believers, and thus we cannot imagine how the Christian story works: that in Jesus, God meets us in our ontological and existential dislocations, and thereby gives us a sense of place, in God. Instead, given our own dislocations, God has become remote, and our sense of homelessness in the universe intensifies the remoteness of God. Yet I also want to suggest that this fact opens up a theological opportunity to reconsider our fundamental understanding of God, and of ourselves, and invites new understandings of divine and human fidelity. For it could be the case that "dislocation" belongs to the very nature of the God who is revealed in the history of Israel, in the Incarnation, and in the Christian dispensation, and that to believe in this God is to come to terms with our own radical dislocation in the universe and even on the earth. This belief, in turn, illumines a sense of "state," not a fixed point, but a spiritual location in relation to God's providential grace that makes of us disciples. And this state of being in relation to God's providence gives us the wherewithal, the stance, from which to enter into solidarity with those who find themselves in various situations of dislocation—human beings suffering and dying, yet grasping for hope. For it is there, in such situations, that we will find the dislocated God once again, and in a certain sense, come home to ourselves.

* * *

This book is written quite frankly for people of struggling faith who live in the kind of world I happen to inhabit, in what has become something of a vast desert called Silicon Valley—a name whose ugliness evokes the spiritual sterility that it has bred, and a concomitant dehumanization and desacralizing of life. God seems distant here, unmoored or untethered from the world around us. But it is we who are dislocated. I suspect that the kind of situation I am describing extends beyond the geographical boundaries of Silicon Valley, California. It could well be that the difficulty to believe that faith could make any difference correlates with the development of political and economic systems, as well as modern and post-Enlightenment thought over the past four hundred years, and the development of science and technology into governing paradigms and epistemes. But given the advent of globalization, it could also well be the case that the situation I am describing and addressing has correlates, forms of experience and expression, in developing and non-Western parts of the world—the majority world. I will not presume, however, that the challenges facing belief in the Western world translate readily into other contexts, cultures, or religious constructs.

More particularly, this book arises from over thirty years of teaching searching (and occasionally bored) undergraduates, and others like them who are reasonably educated and questioning not simply their faith, but whether there are any grounds for committing themselves to believing in anything at all. Given much recent data about the waning of the Christian faith among the young,[1] we could say that today, more than ever, a new approach to considering the things of faith is needed. When I started teaching, I was facing a very different kind of student than the students of today: personal computers were just beginning to appear on the scene, the world was still locked in a Cold War, climate change had not yet emerged as a global concern, global terrorism was as yet unimaginable (much less a 9/11), and the church was in the midst of what would become one of the longest, most defining papacies in history, that of John Paul II. A pope like Francis was far from everyone's imagination then, except as a nostalgia among those old enough to remember of the hope-filled papacy of John XXIII. Although the "modern" world had in fact long since ended and the Western world was in the midst of a "postmodern" phase, and despite the advent of political, liberation, and feminist theologies, the vectors of theological study were still set by the great European theologians of the mid-twentieth century: Barth, Tillich, Rahner, Congar, and other "giants" of that era. Liberation theology was still gaining ground. An introductory course in Catholic theology, or in theological foundations, was a fairly straightforward project because the fundamental vectors of systematic theology had remained unchallenged by the contexts within which students were actually living. Then, as now, some of the most vexing questions had to do with internal church issues such as reception of church teaching on moral matters.

Theology could still be pursued with relatively little attention paid to its historical contextualization, socioeconomic realities, changing gender gestalts, or the realities of religious pluralism. What mattered in the end was whether students emerged from the course with an adequate grasp of some of the fundamentals of Catholic faith and a clear understanding of the questions and issues underlying classic nodal points like the teachings of the Councils of Nicea and Chalcedon, along with other landmarks of the history of Christianity. But, again, all of this was done without adverting in a methodological way to the contexts within which theology students were living and whence they came, much less in any serious way to historical consciousness.

Although the classic and fundamental subject matter, the content of faith, remains essential to a first course in theology, a noncontextualized approach is no longer viable. As Karl Rahner, Roger Haight, Elizabeth Johnson, and other theologians have insisted, we must at the very least take into account the historical consciousness of those who undertake the study of theology or the attempt to understand Christian faith. But this entails attention to the contexts out of which students emerge today, not only in the developed world, but in world that is shared through the globalization of technology and communication. For the students of our day have come of age in the midst of several concurrent dislocations, known not only in the United States, but globally, that have changed the landscape within which we live and within which theology must be developed. Each of these dislocations, in turn, reflects difficulty in locating God within contemporary cultural landscapes. And thus these contexts become theological loci—the points of departure for and frameworks within which we undertake fresh approaches to understanding the God who is the "matter" of Christian faith.

Today, for example, tens of thousands of undocumented Central American youths have crossed the border into the United States, fleeing from violence and hopeless poverty in Honduras, Guatemala, and El Salvador. Some arrived at Nogales, Arizona, which I visited in the course of my preparation of this book. There one beholds a picture of humanity—wretched humanity—in motion. Each day busloads of undocumented migrants—men, women, and children—are discharged at a carefully guarded funnel in the miles-long metal wall that separates the United States from Mexico. Many of them do not even know where they have been deposited. They have nothing more than a knapsack on their backs and, if they are lucky, the temporary resources of NGOs such as the Kino Border Initiative to help get them oriented in a new and unknown country. Families are separated—mothers from children, husbands from wives—and they are left to their wits to figure out how to survive and how to reunite with one another across thousands of miles of land and a bewildering thicket of bureaucracy. This is a picture that has analogues across the globe: Moroccan refugees attempting to find refuge on the island of Lampedusa, meeting a terrifying and watery death in the high seas; Bangladeshi Muslims fleeing poverty and flooding, surging into the crowded streets of Kolkata; Muslims from Eastern China flooding into Shanghai and Beijing; South Sudanese refugees crowding into Nairobi. And, of course, the several millions of Syrian refugees fleeing for their lives into Jordan, Turkey, and Europe. The entire world seems to be in motion, criss-crossing the globe and even within the borders of established nation-states.[2] A visit to almost any of the world's great megalopolises will reveal instantly the results of all this motion—a commingling of peoples of different ethnic, religious, and cultural backgrounds on a scale unprecedented in recorded history.

But this very fact of physical dislocation, brought about by politico-economic upheavals, usually accompanied by the eruption of violence and massive poverty, challenges easy answers to what kind of God is presiding over this sea of human political and social change. As the children of Muslim immigrants live in the same communities as those from Laos and Guatemala in places like California and Texas, there can be no easy or unquestioned assumptions made about "God"—either what kind of God it is we are speaking of or where God is to be located in the midst of this experience. Students who worship Allah sit side by side with students who worship Jesus, and both the Christians and the Muslims sit side by side with students who worship no god—all breathing the same air, following the same sports teams, consuming the same fast food, tracking the same programs on Hulu.

Many students sitting in my classrooms are the products of this kind of motion and human intermingling. They bring to the classroom not a single and largely Caucasian American Catholic middle-class view of the world, but a multiperspectival positioning, as they themselves are often the children of many motions, reflected in their mixed ethnic, cultural, and religious heritages. Now, more than ever, those who self-identify as Catholic present a truly catholic spectrum of understandings and approaches to their faith. In this era of massive political explosions resulting in so much human dislocation, faith in the God disclosed in the person of Jesus can seem to have lost its bearings. The God of Christian faith becomes one god among many, dislocated along with those who are in migration through this life, unmoored from any one cultural or political framework within which "He" previously functioned and over which he presided.

And so the question for Christians is how to believe in such an unmoored God. This will call for some exploration, starting with the sense of "homelessness" on the earth where we (ironically) find ourselves dwelling. The beginning of an answer will come from that common ground shared by all who have been thus dislocated—in our common witness to the impoverishment of the majority of humanity.

Many students today are aware that poverty is the root cause of a great deal of the dislocation they witness in massive migrations. They are also more aware of the great disparities between the rich and the poor that characterize our world than were students of the past. Much of this awareness is the result of reporting by the media, but equally, if not more, social media has connected students with their peers worldwide. It is easy now to gain knowledge of life in places other than the suburban islands of North America. And even among students of relatively slender means, and not only in the United States, travel to distant places is more common than it once was—no longer the academic tourism of a stint in Paris or London, but long-term field work in Burkina Faso, El Salvador, India, or Nepal.

What this means is that today's student comes to theology with a working awareness of the unequal contours of the larger world, which is reflected ever more sharply within the United States and

Europe. One of the biggest questions for these students is how the virtue of solidarity can become a lived reality. They seek not only an abstract theory of solidarity that might assuage a guilty liberal conscience, but a lived kinship that entails a deeper conversion of life, reflected in fundamental decisions about how their lives are to be lived in a world of social and economic dislocation.[3]

The question about God, therefore, arises from a complex of political upheavals, resulting in migrations and intermingling of peoples on an unprecedented scale in human history, and a keen awareness of the reach of global poverty and disease that cry out for a shared response, a solidarity with the victims of history. This is one of the chief loci, then, for a Christian theology today, and constitutes the locus of the first part of my theological exploration.

In Christian theological terms, this line of questioning entails what is meant by faith, and indeed by God, in Christian terms, and how this God can come to be known (i.e., how God is revealed in the midst of dislocation). And so I also ask what it means to have faith, to "believe" in an unmoored God in such times of massive dislocation. This in turn opens up the meaning of God as an abiding and self-giving, ever-creating community of interpersonal love—a God of accompaniment such as we find disclosed in the Hebrew Scriptures. This view of God has real implications for how we can live together, in what ancient Israel called covenant, and how we address a world of such want and poverty. All of this questioning comes together in the person of Jesus, who is God's self-gift to and within a world in commotion. And so this line of questioning also asks who this Jesus is for Christian faith and imagination, and what are the ethical implications of living in his Spirit. Here we are led to a consideration of faith as ecclesial, in the sense of its taking shape within a communion of disciples living in the polis of the world.

Why concern ourselves with the matter of context here? Is it still important that students come away with an understanding of Nicea and Chalcedon? Yes, absolutely. But we must attend to the contexts within which these monuments of the faith tradition are being received, read, and understood today so that what they most deeply concern, the mystery of God revealed in Jesus Christ and in the Gospel—the "scandal of particularity"—might be rendered in the language and forms intelligible to contemporary ears. For what is at stake is not simply assent to beliefs, but the viability of faith, believing in an active sense that makes a difference in and for the world in its particularities. For I am maintaining in this book that a first run in theology must not only take these dislocating factors into account in presenting the Christian theological tradition, but that Christian theology must attend directly to these dislocations in its systematic organization. Why? Because these are not simply historical descriptors, phenomenologies of context: they indicate more fundamental dislocations of God vis-à-vis the postmodern mind and experience. Theology today needs to attend to this divine and human dislocation if it is going to be able to communicate adequately and more fully comprehend the core of Christian faith. Only then can we arrive at some sort of systematic theological organization. It is within that systematic organization that the importance of the "axiomatic" material of a first course in theology can then become clear.

* * *

This book also emerges from personal experience, quandaries, and questions. I am a priest in the Roman Catholic Church and a member of the Society of Jesus. One might think that believing would therefore present few questions to someone such as myself. But that is hardly the case, for commitment itself does not relieve us of the human condition as it is. I, along with everyone else, breathe the air of this world and struggle to make sense of all the often conflicting ways of making sense of reality. This is true as well of the reality of God, the God who has been revealed in Jesus Christ. By no means is it a simple matter to say what it means to believe in this God, or who this God is in whom I am placing my trust. That is why addressing the challenges to belief is a theological matter, for it takes the Christian into the heart of what theologian Karl Rahner called the Holy Mystery that is God. Yet the Mystery is no simple matter. Rilke's poem, quoted at the beginning of this chapter, rings true here:[4] for we are no longer in childhood—not in the current age—and believing in God is no longer a simple matter for many people.

The challenge to belief is also wrought up with the institutions of religion themselves, summed up in what Catholics call "the Church." The advent of modernity brought with it a great centralization of institutions, which, together with technology, led to the development of highly efficient organizations with their own lexicon, dogmas, and "branding" techniques. One could say that this began in earnest for what is today called the Roman Catholic Church in the wake of the Reformation, when religious identity in the modern sense first emerged. People who all along had considered themselves followers of the Catholic faith, the religion of the West rooted in Rome but locally realized and expressed, were now given, and in time appropriated, a distinctive identifying moniker, "Roman Catholic," that distinguished them from other Christians. As modern centralization and technological efficiency intensified, the Roman Catholic Church became more and more publicly recognized as an institution in its own right, with its own sources of revenue and avenues of expenditure, its own internal and external relations, its own polity, law, and politics. After the 1929 Concordat with Italy, in fact, the Vatican became, in effect, the "capital" not only of the Vatican City State, but of a global institution. Rome was again "*capita mundi*," but in a new, ultramodern sense. Now Rome, and more particularly, the Vatican, was linked more than ever with the centralized and bureaucratized authority of a modern institution, and after 1870 and the definition of infallibility at Vatican I in *Pastor Aeternis*, with the personal authority of the head of that institution. Along with this came the modern development of the "Roman Magisterium" in a sense that could not have been imagined in the first century.

It is perhaps not surprising that the institution of the Roman Catholic Church has itself become a stumbling block for some, not least the young, even for believing in God, because the church itself, in the institution of the Roman Magisterium, has claimed to interpret and teach authoritatively, and at times beyond question, what God has revealed. The ironic harvest of modernity, however, is the loss of faith in such institutional claims, whether from churches or from other institutions. When the authority of the institution begins to fade, however, so too can the power of its inner life, that which fuels and sustains belief in God—or in a God who has been so strongly correlated with the authority and traditions of the institution as such. We must add to this analysis, of course, the slippage in symbolic symbol systems, and the collapse of what philosopher Paul Ricoeur called "primary naiveté" in the age of modernity, when what was once held dear has been placed under the microscope of critical analysis and consequent doubt: "Something has been lost, irremediably lost: immediacy of belief."[5]

That said, I would like to make clear that the impetus for this book is not life in the Roman Catholic Church itself, and that this book does not focus on the teaching authority of the church—the magisterium and its various practices. Yes, the church can offer obstacles to faith, or at least to the fervor of faith, and hence to believing. But it seems to me that one of the pitfalls for Catholic thinkers, certainly Catholic theologians, is to begin with the church, and particularly with the church's teaching authority, and some of the issues that occasionally arise there. Catholics can all too easily conflate occasional frustrations with the magisterium, and especially disagreement with its teachings or alienation from the institution, with their posture toward faith itself, and their deeper habits of believing. Theology thus becomes an exercise in "ecclesiasticism"—an obsession with the church as an institution—which is hardly ecclesiology. This is the focus of many popular articles and blogs that focus on the church's politics, personalities, and positions on various topics of interest energizing a few (such as "religious freedom," abortion law, or the latest version of the Roman missal). In the grip of that kind of single-minded obsessiveness, the end of our believing, which is the mystery of God enveloping our lives, can be lost. The purity of religious ideology replaces the mystery of faith. And many, especially the young, choose not to engage at all.

The focus here is on something prior to the church—the human situation that is the result of ontological, existential, and spiritual dislocations, and how we can come to a fresh understanding of God in light of these dislocations. For believing is not only a matter for "churched" people—it is a pervasive problem for anyone who is really living in this world of the massive epistemic, moral, and spiritual shifts that have taken place in the last century. The rise of "the secular" and its various attendant discourses is perhaps only the latest way of trying to get a handle on what has happened and what constitutes our current situation.

What "people of faith" need, or seek, is a deeper grounding in that which they profess to hold. Movements of spirituality in recent times probably signal such a desire for a movement to deeper ground—something beyond mere adherence to a set of beliefs, even those enshrined in the Creed recited weekly at Mass. People wish to plunge deeper into the mystery of the God they profess yet cannot locate. In the early church, this plunge was given the name "mystagogy" or entrance into the mysteries of faith—inaugurating a life of believing through living and breathing one's faith. I am searching here, then, for a renewed mystagogy of believing—one that will take us beyond the divides of faith and reason, and certainly beyond ecclesiasticism, into a lived "practice" of believing: to rediscover the intimacy that is believing, an intimacy revealed in the *cor ad cor loquitur* ("heart speaks unto heart")of the Incarnation, where God and human beings enter into the pattern of address and response. It is this intimacy, this "spirituality" if you will, that I think we seek today, and that lies at the heart of belief, certainly belief in God.

* * *

THE PLAN OF THIS BOOK

The way toward a God who has become so dislocated and unmoored from our experience is to come to terms with our own sense of dislocation—or dislocations—some of which have been brought about by our efforts to engage the ineffable. In reflecting on the suffering of dislocation, one is reminded of the story of Jacob, who was himself radically dislocated by God, even physically debilitated in his nocturnal struggle with God, who, in the form of an angel, fought to enter into Jacob's heart (Gn 32:24–32). In that particular struggle, Jacob survived, although he himself was left maimed, his thigh seemingly dislocated from his hip. When Jacob asks the "man" (angel) his name, he receives a reply that echoes the enigmatic divine reply to Moses's similar question before the burning bush (Ex 4:13–14): "Why is it that you ask my name?" God remains ineffable. That struggle with the ineffable God is our own struggle as well. It is from nights of interior struggle that anything like believing in God will emerge. Chapter 1, then, treats of what we can say about knowing God at this moment in human history and explores more deeply what it means to say that God has become "dislocated" with respect to human life and existence, unmoored from previous bearings. This raises the broader question of believing, and why believing today is more difficult than it might have been in a time when God seemed more a part of the overall picture for humanity. Yet, as I wish to claim, the inability to comprehend, even the loss of a sense of God, can in fact be understood as an intrinsic moment in the experience of God.

Chapter 2 delves yet more deeply into the problem of believing today, casting it in terms of the existential "homelessness" experienced by people in the world today. We are speaking of a form of disorientation that results from a displacement from oneself—from one's sense of "being at home" in the world, even in the cosmos. The disruptions of the imagination that the discovery of heliocentrism in early modernity imposed on philosophical and theological magisteria were just the beginning of a path leading toward a sense of homelessness in the universe as a whole and to thoughts of existential meaninglessness. One reaction, however, was that a new "Promethean man" (Nietzsche's *Übermensch*—a far cry from the maimed Jacob) claimed his own place in defiance of his having been dislodged from the center. Perhaps in this Nietzschean spirit, though Nietzsche lived in the nineteenth century, the earlier philosophical disruptions and paradigm shifts of the seventeenth century were to usher in a modern world of scientific thinking, economic planning, and a refashioning of the human experience through trade systems that would result in dislocations of entire peoples, including twenty million African slaves, hundreds of millions of itinerant works in our time, as well as millions of refugees and homeless persons around the globe. The question would become how we can begin to imagine God in the face of the kind of suffering epitomized by the literal dislocation of millions of people across the planet—on city sidewalks, in refugee camps, on boats in the high seas, crossing borders—all of them homeless, not only in the universe, but on planet Earth itself, and at the hands of other human beings. In a sense, these dislocated human beings represent all of us, even as they cry out for our help, our solidarity. Yet serious questions are raised about God, about God's involvement in our fate, and how we can begin to imagine that involvement.

If we are to rediscover a believing in God, then the God we need to imagine is most likely not an omnipotent titan, nor only a compassionate overseer, but rather one who has suffered a divine dislocation—or allowed a kind of divine suffering in the self-gift that we find in Jesus of Nazareth. Chapter 3 discusses the divine self-emptying, or *kenosis* (Phil 2:1–12)—that act of love deriving from the inner life of God that results in the dislocation of God from the heavenly places. This divine dislocation is, in a sense, the "answer" to the cries for help from suffering humanity, the homelessness of humanity. The Incarnation is the way by which God moves outside of God's own sphere, God's fixed throne, and into the chaos of all forms of human dislocation. The dislocation of God who is disclosed in Jesus suffers with humanity and undergoes a true death. This kenotic movement discloses not only who the human is, but who God is, and in light of who God is, more deeply yet what constitutes human nature. It therefore unfurls a revelation not only about God but about humanity, with implications for all dimensions of human existence, both spiritual and embodied, personal and political. I focus here on one dimension of what is revealed about dislocated humanity—poverty—in both its literal and spiritual senses, as a key to understanding all aspects of the human, including death. For it is in the poverty of our humanity, including the poverty of our sinfulness, that we can behold just how dislocated we are, and how radically near God in fact has come by entering into this state.

Jesus, born into the poverty of radical dislocation, shows by his person, in his words and deeds, what it means to follow in the pathways of a dislocated God. This means, first of all, entering into solidarity with those whose suffering generates so much uprootedness and dislocation, both existential and spiritual. Chapter 4 considers what such solidarity might mean and theological foundations for undertaking it. I turn here to the work of liberation theologian Jon Sobrino, for whom solidarity takes the form of what he calls "the praxis of Resurrection" or "taking the crucified down from their crosses." He proposes this image as the fundamental mode of solidarity for Christians today, with all of those who are suffering in the world. It is in that solidarity, with the "crucified peoples," that we will find God—a God who has become otherwise lost to us. As others have shown so eloquently, this solidarity with the dislocated of history is what moved Salvadoran Archbishop Oscar Romero, the Jesuit martyrs of El Salvador, the Cistercian monks of Atlas, and countless others in history to witness in solidarity with the dislocated, even giving up their lives in solidarity, as did Jesus. Martyrdom is a key to understanding faith and what it means to believe—the real difference that it makes in a human life.

Yet no such witness is isolated and solitary. Such solidarity stands within the folds of a "cloud of witnesses" who constitute the larger reality of the church. The focus of chapter 5 is the meaning of lived faith, even before we begin to speak of the church as an institution. How would our imagining a world of such perpetual instability, of ongoing motion, of pilgrimage, lead to a different understanding of faith, and then of the church, of its mission, and of our places within it? How can the church understand itself in a radical way as a dislocated people in solidarity with the dislocated of the Earth, and indeed with the Earth itself, this tiny garden afloat in the cosmos? And what would be the concrete, lived, implications be for the church of taking to heart a praxis of radical solidarity? For those who follow in the way of Jesus, or try to, discipleship names an intrinsic moment in the life of a faith that is an ongoing experience of dislocation, of moving outside of and beyond one's zones of familiarity and comfort. Discipleship draws the disciple into solidarity with the suffering, into solidarity with the God who has suffered dislocation so as to meet us in our suffering, and most particularly into a solidarity that is in itself witness to the ineffable Mystery. Chapter 5, then, explores the meaning of discipleship as this ongoing movement of displacement, of dislocating oneself for the sake of what Jesus called the Reign of God.

In the epilogue I return to the problem with which the book begins and suggest that a retrieval of belief and of a sense of location vis-à-vis God can be found in what I am calling a "mystagogy of believing," where the "content" of faith is realized in the living of it. Here we consider believing in light of the mystery of God, a gift that, as theologian Jean-Luc Marion has helped us to understand, saturates us to the point of occupying no space, fixing no attention, attracting no gaze. The problem posed at the outset is now turned on its head: the divine dislocation is not the problem; it is our failure to begin to comprehend that this God without fixity is the very God we have claimed all along. "God becomes invisible not in spite of givenness but by virtue of that givenness."[6] This, in turn, is not so much a stumbling block to believing, but an entrée into believing, and believing with joy, in a God who has no location, and who is always present in the midst of our own dislocation.

1

The Problem of Believing in a Dislocated God

I shall be there as who I am shall I be there.
—Exodus 3:14
Rendering of the Hebrew
by John Courtney Murray,
The Problem of God, Yesterday and Today

He began to leave Us!
Bored with His Angels, Bewitched by Humanity,
In Mortifying imitation of You, his least creation,
He would sail off on Voyages, no knowing where
. . . BEYOND US.

—Tony Kushner
Angels in America

The story of Moses is oddly reassuring—*reassuring* because God makes an appearance, and *oddly* because, nevertheless, God remains elusive. The one who remains elusive still reassures us with a presence. Yet something seems to have happened between the days of the burning bush, when God's presence was palpable to the people of Israel, and the present time; God seems not only elusive but to have floated off. Tony Kushner captured it well in his major contribution to American drama, written at the height of the AIDS crisis in the United States. Speaking of God, the Angel laments, "He began to leave us . . . no knowing where . . . BEYOND US"—a familiar sensibility by many who witness the meaninglessness of suffering and the power of evil in our world. God has disappeared from the scene, or so it seems. We are left alone, the void created by the divine absence filled with confusion and darkness, and our own grappling with the tragedies that befall us.

Why does this seem to be the case for so many people today?

A WARY AGE

We live in a wary age, an age that has been stung enough that people are cautious. Confidence in religion has weakened while God has slipped to the margins of everyday consciousness; believing has diminished, and in some places has disappeared. The way we understand the world has changed. The order and boundaries of the old dispensation have given way to uncertainty and ambiguity. Charles Taylor has summed it up as well as anyone can.

> The present scene, shorn of the earlier forms, is different and unrecognizable to any earlier epoch. It is marked by an unheard of pluralism of outlooks, religious and non- and anti-religious, in which the number of possible positions seems to be increasing without end. It is marked in consequence by a great deal of . . . movement between different outlooks. It naturally depends on one's milieu, but it is harder and harder to find a niche where either belief or unbelief go without saying. And as a consequence, the proportion of belief is smaller and that of unbelief is larger than ever before.[1]

The "wary" of this "wary age" include the so-called "nones," people who claim no belief whatsoever, and for whom religion, much less God, is not on the table—at least not in the ways that have been presented through the formal doctrinal traditions of Christianity. Some nones, though not all, may say, "I'm spiritual, but not religious," while others may pursue a purely secularist path through life, at least for now. But these are simply the youngest exemplars of what Taylor has called "the buffered self," for whom the churches and their doctrines no longer serve as unifying agents for religious and moral life, and for whom "the spiritual as such is no longer intrinsically related to society."[2] One result is that the presence of God has disappeared from our constructs of the cosmos, as well as from moral and civic polity.[3]

The category of the wary also includes people who might describe themselves as questioning. They struggle with their belief, partly because of the nature of the world we live within, and partly because the institutions that once transmitted the traditions of faith have largely lost their ability to convince. A series on National Public Radio, "Losing Our Religion," described what is going on among the younger generations in the United States, where belief in God is waning.[4] Many people, not only the young, yearn to believe in something not just greater than themselves, providing a sense of meaning, but in a transcendent source of hope. The radio program captured one young person's proto-nostalgia for such a believing, in God:

> I don't [believe in God] but I really want to. . . . I think having a God would create a meaning for our lives, like we're working toward a purpose—and it's all worthwhile because at the end of the day we will maybe move on to another life where everything is beautiful. I love that idea.

This is a poignant expression of desire for something that eludes many people today: the experience of some kind of orientation toward the transcendent. For the God who was once familiar, because God was "locatable" in a religious geography and scientific cosmology, is no longer easily found. The God who was once situated in a known universe of meaning and reference has moved elsewhere. Some people can no longer believe, much as they might yearn to believe, because, as in the cry of Kushner's angel, God is no longer present for them. Not only are they themselves dislocated, "homeless" in the universe; God too, has become dislocated.[5]

A GOD UNMOORED—BUT WHICH GOD?

Which God is at stake when we speak of the dislocation of God, and of those who were once believers? To begin with, there is the God of modern theism, often presumed in debates about God's existence, and so ably described by Elizabeth Johnson:

> This view envisions God on the model of a monarch at the very peak of the pyramid of being. Without regard for Christ or the Spirit, it focuses on what Trinitarian theology would call the "first person," a single powerful individual who dwells on high, ruling the cosmos and judging human conduct. Even when this Supreme Being is portrayed with a benevolent attitude, which the best of theology does, "He," for it is always the ruling male who stands for this idea, is essentially remote. At times he intervenes to affect the laws of nature and work miracles, at times not. Although he loves the world, he is uncontaminated by its messiness. And always this distant lordly lawgiver stands at the summit of hierarchical power, reinforcing structures of authority in society, church and family.[6]

This widely held view of God is certainly the view rejected by modern atheism. But it also supersedes a very different notion of God, one that derives from the Bible: the mysterious God of Abraham and Sarah, of the burning bush, and of Jesus.[7] The problem is that the rejection of the God of theism has for very many included the rejection of the God of Abraham. That God—the God of Abraham, Isaac, and Jacob—no longer seems to encounter us.

How did this come about? The larger framework of the problem can be understood if we look at two main cultural shifts in the West: the development out of the Christian West of a secular society and its implications for believing, and the gradual dissociation of faith from reason that resulted in a gulf between the claim of having faith and believing in God. Taylor has recast the meaning of the secular and of secularity's impact on religious belief and takes a new look at the standard "secularity thesis" that has been a staple of intellectual history of the West since the seventeenth century.

> From the seventeenth century on, a new possibility gradually arose: a conception of social life in which the "secular" was all there was. Since "secular" originally referred to profane or ordinary time, in contradistinction to higher times, what

was necessary was to come to understand profane time without any reference to higher times.[8]

The so-called "secularity thesis" sees the emergence of science in the seventeenth and eighteenth centuries in particular not only as a matter of knowing the world (an epistemic event), but as a ground-shifting event (an ontological event), meaning that the entire cultural, religious, and metaphysical framing of what human beings in the West considered to be real underwent a radical revision. The requirements for what would count as "real" depended increasingly on empirical description, if not verification, and the "hypothesis of God" increasingly seemed no longer necessary to understand this narrow rendering of reality. Indeed, belief in God soon became an intellectual option, and with that option, atheism grew in its plausibility.

The move toward the secular, Taylor argues, is partly owing to the loss of an "enchanted" world that once governed both daily human life and the faith that imbued it. By this he means a world that was once populated by spirits, both good and bad, and by their attendant magic. This was the world that obtained in premodern times. But a process of disenchantment, certainly fueled in part by the rise of modern science and shifts away from premodern social arrangements to the rise of the modern state, brought about a view of the world that no longer depended on such an imaginative construct. Along with disenchantment, then, there arose a world in which it was no longer necessary to believe in the unseen (the *invisibilium*). God receded to the margins of reality, first as a force, and then as an idea.[9] This was an epistemic shift, to be sure, but also one of moral and spiritual sensibility and significance. "The process of disenchantment, which involved a change in us, can be seen as the loss of a certain sensibility, which is really an impoverishment."[10] And with the revolutions of the eighteenth century, Western modernity became "very inhospitable to the transcendent."[11] Religious belief and religious imagination were thereby gradually relegated to the sphere of pious opinion. Human beings were consigned to the sphere of earthly immanence and an attendant loss of God.

German philosopher Jürgen Habermas sees the nature of the

secular differently, tracing it to the rupture in the relationship between faith and reason, which had been united in the medieval consensus. With the rise of science as the governing paradigm for understanding reality—what we could term a postmetaphysical scientism—the synthesis between faith and reason that had obtained in the premodern world, "the tradition extending from Augustine to Thomas fell apart."[12] The result for religion was a discarding of the former notion of sacred knowledge (the wisdom accrued from Scripture, religious tradition, theology, and philosophy, all bound together in a common metaphysics) in favor of a suprarational knowledge that did not rest on such traditional foundations. In some cases, such as various forms of fundamentalism, religion even entered into the realm of the irrational, while a secular rationality, often rooted in a faith in scientific method ("scientism") assumed the sole mantle of reason. But now, Habermas claims, things have changed: We are living in what he calls a "postsecular" era, one that coincides with the resurgence of religion, and not only in the West. This is a time of recalibration of the categories of sacred and secular and of how they relate to each other. While the secular stands on its own, and has requirements for knowledge that the religious interlocutor must respect, the secularist nonetheless must acknowledge the bona fide contribution to overall knowledge and understanding of the human condition that religion has offered and can offer even now.

> It makes a difference whether we speak with one another or merely about one another. If we want to avoid the latter, two presuppositions must be fulfilled: the religious side must accept the authority of "natural" reason as the fallible results of the institutionalized sciences and the basic principles of universalistic egalitarianism in law and morality. Conversely, secular reason may not set itself up as the judge concerning truths of faith, even though in the end it can accept as reasonable only what it can translate into its own, in principle universally accessible, discourses.[13]

A secularist dismissal of religion cannot easily be sustained in the contemporary world situation, despite the temptation to dismiss religion peremptorily. But a religious dismissal of secularist ways of construing the world is equally unsustainable.

Moving beyond Habermas, Saudi-born anthropologist Talal Asad deconstructs the categories of the sacred (or religious) and the secular altogether. His framing is neither epistemological nor metaphysical, but rather anthropological. The secular is a "concept that brings together certain behaviors, knowledges, and sensibilities in modern life."[14] It is not a singular or stable notion: "The secular, I argue, is neither continuous with the religious that supposedly preceded it . . . nor a simple break from it."[15] Nor is the religious a fixed category. The history of the "sacred" and of the "secular" does not follow a grand narrative resulting in the inexorable triumph of the secular (the secularity thesis), where the secular serves as a "mask" for religion, serving a quasi-religious function of providing an all-encompassing and coherent worldview. In the West, at least, these two notions depend on each other, and each produces its own myths: the liberal secularist myth and the redemptive myth of Christianity. The myths themselves jostle with each other for primary space, with the situating of the Christian god in a supernatural world, much like the god of theism described by Johnson. But for Asad, these myths are powerful in their own right in shaping worldviews:

> The question of whether people did or did not believe in these ancient narratives . . . does not quite engage with the terrain that mythic discourse inhabited in this culture. For the sacred did not function as a single totalizing myth structure in pre-modern discourses. Instead there were disparate places, objects, and times, each with its qualities, and each requiring conduct and words appropriate to it.[16]

If anything, the situation that Asad describes is closer to our own situation than the version offered by the standard secularity thesis that the secular is the result of the triumph of a scientific worldview that displaced the sacred. For even in the midst of an overwhelmingly secular milieu, we have witnessed the rise and resurgence of religious movements, both benign and fearsome, that belie a simple binary construction of a reality split between the religious and the secular. And, even among those who claim some religious faith, the mythological and symbolic structures of those religious faiths, including those of Catholicism, have various and tenuous holds, or are mixed with other mythic and symbolic systems from other religions. This is happening even as these very same religious people negotiate life in a world where none of these myths have any real power within everyday technocratic society. Believing then becomes less a matter of intellectual assent to doctrines and beliefs than a congeries of practices and rituals that include a wide spectrum of expressions. This notion of believing creates wide space for intellectual, social, and ethical engagement between believers and nonbelievers.

Still, there remains the fact of the gradual dissociation of faith from reason that would create a tension between faith and what people believe, a topic treated by Pope Emeritus Benedict XVI in his controversial Regensburg Address of September 12, 2006, "Faith, Reason, and the University: Memories and Reflections."[17] The main point of that address was the "rapprochement between Biblical faith and Greek philosophical inquiry." What Pope Benedict wished to convey is that there resides in revelation itself, indeed in the revelation of God to Moses as well as in the Christian revelation of God in Jesus Christ, a role for logos, rationality, and reason, all lying at the heart the revelation. Christian revelation is not some arational or even irrational set of "religious experiences" that was later given a philosophical framework through the encounter of the Palestinian Jesus movement with currents of Greek thought—a variant of the thesis put forward by Adolf von Harnack in his influential work *The History of Dogma*. Contrary to those who would argue that the rationality of the story of salvation arrived subsequent to the revelation itself as part of a Hellenizing process, Benedict argues that logos is so inherently bound up with the divine revelation that to fail to enact faith with and through reason is to act contrary to God's nature—a view congruent with natural law, which holds that what has been revealed is accessible to reason because it has been inscribed by a rational God. The uncoupling of God and logos, he argued, is not only a trait of certain strands of Islam but also major aberrations of Christian faith in the history of Christianity where reason has given way to ideology or to irrationality and violence. This process, which the pope saw as a result of the wedge driven between faith and reason as a result of secularization, can also result in a religion of mere "feeling," where faith and belief become matters of opinion untethered from reason.[18] When religion degenerates into ideology or irrationality, then belief, understood as a rational assent to truth, becomes problematic at best.

THE PROBLEM OF RELIGION ITSELF

What I have been saying, in essence, is that religion itself has become a problem for contemporary Western people. The "New Atheists" of the past decade are only the more obvious and influential voices, for there is a well-established bedrock of the alienation of intellectuals from religion.[19] But the distrust of religious institutions is broadly shared, not only by intellectuals but by broad swaths of people in contemporary secularized societies. As a result, religion in general has come under intense scrutiny; media-endorsed authors and television pundits express alienation from religion, if not outright mockery of religious belief.[20] It is easy for people who struggle with religious belief to find themselves resentful of the dismissal meted out to religion when the grounds for dismissal can seem quite shallow, both rhetorically and intellectually. Yet people of religious conviction would do well to ask why this happening. For underlying this posture toward religion is a series of massive shifts—epistemological, scientific, economic, political, social, and religious—that have made room for this kind of critique.

Moreover, it must be said that religion itself can be and has been its own worst enemy. There is the chronicle of wars and hatreds through the centuries, and now the further evidence of religion's dark side: the abuse of religion that led to September 11 and its aftermath, the distortions of Islam by ISIS and other extremists, the distortions of Buddhism and of Hinduism by so-called "fundamentalists," and, in another realm, the handling of the sex-abuse scandal that has rocked the Roman Catholic Church. And there are so many other examples. The opportunities for criticizing religious belief on the grounds of the failures of religious people and institutions are legion. Like sex and money, religion can redound to tremendous good or spawn great evil.

But the deeper reality that has made possible all of these attacks on religion, many of them well earned, is arguably not the scandal of religion itself. The deeper reality was named by Nietzsche over one hundred years ago: the Western world has suffered a loss of a sense of God, at least the God of theism who had crowned society in earlier times, when a Christendom was the order of the day. Nietzsche's famous scene of the madman in the marketplace still has a ring of truth.

> The madman jumped into their midst and pierced them with his eyes. "Whither is God?" he cried; "I will tell you. We have killed him—you and I. All of us are his murderers. . . . Whither are we moving? Away from all suns? Are we not plunging continually? Backward, sideward, forward, in all directions? Is there still any up or down? Are we not straying as through an infinite nothing? Do we not feel the breath of empty space? . . . Do we hear nothing as yet of the noise of the gravediggers who are burying God? Do we smell nothing as yet of the divine decomposition? . . . God is dead. God remains dead. And we have killed him."[21]

This is not the manifesto of a village atheist; it is the jeremiad of a cultural prophet. Whatever it was that once held Western culture together in a modern consensus, with a rational ordering from bottom to top and a strong sense of transcendent sanction, had disappeared. The madman asked, "Whither are we moving?" because God, who had stood at the pinnacle of this picture, had been "murdered" by the emergence of the autonomous self, the human being pitted against the brute forces of nature and fate, and other human beings. In the nineteenth century it had become clear that the development of a capitalist economy, the replacement of medieval order by nation-states, and the rise of a scientific worldview independent even of a natural philosophy, much less a natural theology, had led to the toppling of God, for God was no friend of this new man and could no longer undergird a social morality.[22]

Theologian Michael J. Buckley has taken this analysis one step further by holding that in the nineteenth century God became the enemy of human nature, Satanic in the sense of representing the antihuman:

> What the dialectical movement of the nineteenth century had come to assert over the earlier theism was actually a Satanic understanding of God, the enemy of the human. God was understood—deconstructed, if you will—as Satan. Christianity was revealed as a destructively parasitic and decadent hostility to human life. To understand the passion, the urgency, even the hatred of the anti-theism that emerged from within that century, it is imperative to understand that—without ever naming it as such—atheistic humanism thought itself in a struggle to eliminate the satanic in human history, the alienation and destruction of the human.[23]

And so, whereas Nietzsche had proclaimed with some cynicism the triumph of petty bourgeois values and religion resulting in the death of God, God soon came to be seen as literally incredible and dispensable—neither necessary nor desired for guaranteeing a rational understanding of the world or of the human being. The very notion of God was threatening to the human person, to human freedom and rationality. God had not only been loosened from human grasp, but also denied, and then willfully "disappeared." The events of the twentieth century in Europe could be interpreted in light of this historical development, where, in effect, the word "God" had been erased, replaced with the systemic idols of nationalism and race. What remained of God was an empty shell, a trace of what had once been palpably present.[24]

But today we are seeing the emergence of something different from the murder of God, much less of an atheism pure and simple. I am not speaking of a formal agnosticism as a position carefully thought out and intellectually confirmed as such. I am speaking, rather, of the aftermath of the death of God, a "post-atheistic" sense of loss—not the sense of loss that comes with death, but the sense of disorientation and emptiness that comes when we no longer have the thoughts or words to put anything together. It is a loss the nature of which we might not even be consciously aware, like the feeling one has on awaking from a dream where everything seemed so clear, but in the waking state one is unable to remember with exactitude all the characters or quite what transpired—a gnawing sense of irretrievable loss. The dream itself belongs to an inaccessible world, one that cannot be completely regained, even with the effort of imagination, intelligence, and the powers of memory.

Much of this sense of loss is contained in the emergence of a philosophical literature today that speaks of the "return" of religion and of the "return" of God. This new line of thinking presupposes that in a postmetaphysical world, it can seem that we do not even have the concepts, much less the language, to recapture God. But God's traces are still to be found, traces from a cultural setting in which a whole metaphysics once buttressed a world of faith in God and articulation of that faith in beliefs. Philosophers such as John Caputo, Gianni Vattimo, and Richard Kearney have endeavored to establish new ways of thinking about faith and belief, ways that do not presuppose the God of traditional metaphysics.[25] Of these, Kearney in particular captures the spirit of the times:

> It is only if one concedes that one knows virtually nothing about God that one can begin to recover the presence of holiness in the flesh of ordinary existence. Such holiness, I will suggest, was always already there—only we didn't see, touch, or hear it. This is what Jacob discovered after he wrestled with the stranger throughout the night, realizing at dawn that he had seen the face of God. It is what the disciples of Jesus discovered after they had walked with the stranger down the road to Emmaus.[26]

What these thinkers succeed in capturing is the fact that for many in the West today, the old bearings are gone, but that perhaps God can be rediscovered if we imagine God anew, in the very midst of our current states of dislocation. Speculative metaphysics of being is replaced by a metaphysics of experience.[27]

Karl Rahner captured the situation of contemporary dislocation in his meditation on the word "God" and what might occur were that word ever forgotten. It is helpful to recall that he was reflecting on this topic in the wake of World War II, when he witnessed firsthand in his own country, Germany, how a forgetting of God, and the replacement of God with a system of idolatry, led to massively tragic consequences.

It might sound strange to ask what would happen if a mere word were forgotten; many words have dropped from the common lexicon. But it is not the word "God" itself that is at issue; the real cause of wonderment is that there is such a word at all. That there is such a word suggests something about the very nature of the human being, the one who has fashioned the word and searches for the referent of the word.[28] The word has arisen in the course of the human experience of transcendence—the search for and moving toward the totality of all that is—an experience that is bound up with and comes to expression in language. Language yields a word that would capture the origin and goal of this transcendence, which has been given the name "God." Yet this is no ordinary word; it is a referent without an object. The word God points to no object as such, but rather to a reality that cannot be fully grasped or known; thus it denotes the ineffable.[29]

Rahner asks what would happen if the word were to be forgotten. That is, what would happen if we were to imagine a species called *homo sapiens* that had lost the experience of transcendence:

> Human beings would forget all about themselves in their preoccupation with all the individual details of their world and their existence. *Ex supposito* they would never face the totality of the world and of themselves helplessly, silently, and anxiously. They would not notice any more that they were only individual existents, and not being as such. . . . They would be mired in the world and in themselves, and no longer go through that mysterious process which they are. . . . Human beings would have forgotten the totality and its ground, and at the same time, if we can put it this way, would have forgotten that they had forgotten. What would it be like? We can only say: they would have ceased being human beings. They would have regressed to the level of clever animals.[30]

The word itself, then, is a reminder of who we are as beings who have the experience of transcendence. Loss of the word, or the "absolute death of the word 'God,' including even the eradication of its past, would be the signal, no longer heard by anyone, that [humanity] itself had died."[31] This is what has happened, in effect, under totalitarian systems but also, it could be argued, under the dominance of technocratic paradigms that render the transcendent superfluous or relegate it condescendingly to the realm of fantasy.

The alternative to such a complete eradication of the word would be its survival, even if that survival is surrounded by argument over its ultimate referent, as it has been at least since the onset of the Enlightenment. But the arguments about the ultimate referent of the word "God" themselves presume what Hans-Georg Gadamer called a "world-view of language"—what makes possible any arguments about god as such.[32] Quite apart from any topic at hand, we regularly and always surrender ourselves to the a priori world of language in which we live, and by which we come to self-consciousness and construct worlds of communication. For we humans do not want to face the terror of an absolute loneliness. The word "God" persists in the world of language because its function within this world is to point to the ineffable totality of the reality within which we stand. And "for this very reason the word 'God' is not just any word, but is the word in which language, that is, the self-expression of the self-presence of the world and human existence together, grasps itself in its ground."[33]

Of course, the actual English word and its Anglo-Saxon antecedents are not precisely what is in question here. But what is at issue is how we are to understand the "loss of God"—as a marker of the human condition, or as a historically conditioned moment that harbors still the possibility for the recovery of belief, perhaps in some new way. For there is still to be found a yearning, a spiritual straining, for what is indicated by the absence, for what has been forgotten. *I have faith, but I am not sure that I believe.* The transcendent aspirations of the human spirit have not been completely deadened; we are not yet mere ciphers of human beings, the ultimate outcome of Rahner's scenario—or at least we hope not. The vast majority of us are also beings who yearn, and in this yearning transcend ourselves, despite our being mired in the finitude of the real. As Rahner maintained, even for those claims that there is ultimately nothing encompassing the cosmos, or sustaining it, or imbuing it—making those claims requires some act of self-transcendence in order to arrive at that conclusion. Even the starkest avowals of atheism are the result of a stepping outside oneself in order to stake such a claim in the first place.

A DISLOCATED GOD FOR A DISLOCATED PEOPLE

If the emergence of the secular explains in part how we can speak of the dislocation of God and how God has become unmoored from the bearings of old, then surely, we are justified in believing that at one stage God could be located—that people could point to a place or a religious superstructure and say, in effect, "God dwells there, in that Holy of Holies"? Yet the history of Israel suggests that a God of such fixed location was not lasting, or perhaps not meant to last, and that, in fact, apart from divine theophanies on holy mountains (e.g., Sinai, Horeb) and sacred sites (e.g., Shechem, Pinuel), the God of Israel is, by virtue of the very divine nature, a dislocated God, a God without fixed place.

Consider the story of the encounter between Moses and the God of Israel in the theophany of the burning bush (Ex 3). Moses himself has been transformed by an encounter with God, and now he is leading a wandering people through the desert, from their Egyptian captivity toward a land of promise. They themselves are radically dislocated—itinerant, homeless refugees. Moses is the perfect example of a human being living in and by faith: one who believed in what he hoped for, convinced that the divine promises would reach fulfillment in an ultimate future (Heb 11:1). Moses seemingly lived in a darkness as he longed to know God and see God's promises fulfilled. Yet precisely because he could not see this God, much less comprehend him, Moses could not attach a name to his God. When he descends the mountain, face glowing, he does not tell his people that he now has an exhaustive understanding of God, for God has not granted him that kind of knowledge. When Moses asks God's name, he is given the enigmatic response, "I am who am" (Ex 3:14). This is a God who, even as an abiding presence, will remain elusive, seemingly absent, and most often silent.

The fuller Hebrew rendering, "I shall be with you as who I am, shall I be there," implies that this God who has heard the cries of his people will be located in the midst of their suffering, not in a fixed place.[34] This God does not yet dwell in a temple; God dwells with his people, and in fact emphasizes that this belongs to his nature: the chosen people come to know this God by letting him enter into the depths of their suffering as they wander through the desert. In this encounter a covenant emerges, a trust in the *'emeth* of the Lord, God's abiding merciful presence in the midst of the people of Israel.[35] Faith in this God emerges as a fragile desert flower, unfolding moment by moment, step by step, as Moses and the wandering people slowly make their way through the trackless shifting sands. This is, as theologian Peter Phan has expressed it, not a fixed God, but a "*Deus Migrator.*"[36] The covenant is an existential commitment that is not buttressed by the assurances of a fixedness of perspective, much less the fixity of a temple. And the Promised Land itself is not so much a land, a place, as it is a horizon of hope that moves with the people, just as God does.

"A wandering Aramaean was my father" (Dt 26:5). God leads and accompanies the people into the desert and into a nomadic existence. While there may be assurances of God's presence—a tower of flame, a looming cloud—and God again and again initiates a covenantal relationship with Israel, Israel's yearning for a fixed place, and a fixed place for God to dwell within, is not to be granted during Moses's lifetime or the lifetime of the chosen people (Heb 13). Instead, they will live in the promise of a people whose ancestors, too, were wanderers.

This pattern is repeated in the transformative experience of the Babylonian exile (597 to 538 BCE), during which waves of the chosen people were deported from Jerusalem into captivity in Babylon. In 586 BCE the First Temple was destroyed. This period is richly recorded in the Psalms, as well as in the Book of Lamentations, which paint the picture of a people forlorn, stripped of the familiar supports of faith, the temple itself destroyed.[37] But out of this harrowing experience came the deeper realization that faith in their God did not depend on being able to locate God in a fixed sanctuary, that precisely in their own dislocation they were discovering that God has no permanent location, and that the only dwelling place of God for this homeless people was in their hearts. "In the exile, then, the people realized that they could turn to God anywhere with the confidence that he would be near, and that he would be their sanctuary in a foreign land."[38] The covenant would now run deeper than ritual observance; it would be inscribed on hearts, both to say and to do (Dt 30:1–15). The temple would be rebuilt, but destroyed again, in 70 CE, resulting in a diaspora for the Jews, a wandering and dislocation that became defining in subsequent centuries.

Believing in such a God is not altogether easy, for believing is a fragile enterprise, one constantly tested through the fatigue of faith, and even the failure of faith. Like love, a person (or a whole people) can fall out of it; one can lose fervor for its object. This is especially the case as one wanders farther and farther from the source—or as a whole people does so, in the case of the chosen people in the desert. The Jews wandering in the desert are people of faith whose convictions waver, and for whom fidelity is a great struggle, one often marked by failure. The history of Israel is marked by episodic rejections of the "I am who am" God of Abraham, Isaac, and Jacob, and there is a turning to all sorts of other ways of understanding the world and their place within it that have more allure under the circumstances: a turn toward idols. The true God is eclipsed, and a living sense of that God lost. It will be Moses's task, and the task of judges and prophets, to work to bring them back, again and again, to a life within the covenant of the only God—to move them from dislocation to a sense of home.

* * *

And that returns us to our moment in history. Many people, such as the young person quoted at the beginning of this chapter, would claim to desire faith, in the sense of aspiring in transcendence toward what they cannot name. I do not have in mind here atheists, but rather, people who were or are in some sense, perhaps in a very explicit sense, religious, but for whom it has become difficult to believe in a final goal (*terminus ad quem*) of their yearning. God is no longer within their grasp. That goal of faith has become for such people increasingly elusive, to the point that it has become difficult if not impossible to name precisely, in an intellectually and emotionally convincing way, where their faith is directed. Some people for whom this is the case have become existential wanderers, lurching from one way station to another—any passing fad that appears under the banner of "spirituality"—but finding no ultimate meaning in these places. For others, the planet itself, if not the cosmos, has become something of a substitute for what cannot be grasped, endowed with its own mysterious depth. They have not, in Rahner's sense, forgotten the word "God," but for some even this word does not adequately express a clear focus of faith. In short, there is a gap, an emptiness—loss—between the aspiration of faith and the content of that faith, what people name as their belief. For some, it is a matter of not being able to give intellectual assent to various doctrines; for others, it is something deeper—a radical doubt about what faith has said all along about who God is. If faith is the "assurance of things hoped for, the evidence of things unseen" (Heb 11:1), then the evidence part, that which pertains to belief, seems to be up for grabs, contested from many different angles, and left unsettled.

All of this is confounded by how we understand believing itself. For the church proposes propositions for our assent, what Roger Haight terms "beliefs"—expressions of an underlying faith in the transcendent.[39] The problem is that, given the way some of these beliefs are formulated or proposed, some people can no longer give full intellectual assent to them or conform to their implications. People may reject lower-order "beliefs" such as various propositions about human sexuality, and also reject both the church and God in the process. But in rejecting beliefs about the God of theism, as Elizabeth Johnson described this understanding of God, do they unwittingly reject the God of Abraham, Isaac, and Jacob, of whom Pascal spoke? The longing for something to anchor love and forgiveness might suggest that they have not. Many people are not given to think very often about the fact that believing is something more profound, much more personal, and entailing far greater degrees of freedom (a form of responsibility) than we might imagine. Believing is not mere assent to propositions; it is more a trusting relationship—to go back to Moses and the chosen people—with a Mystery that leads us to shape our lives in certain ways that make at least an ethical difference to ourselves and to others. But even more, this relationship reveals us to *who* we are: mysteries unto ourselves. All this comes from a relationality with a God whose very nature is to be dislocated, and to be present to us in our own dislocation. Rahner spoke of contemporary Christians in the world as a people thrust into "diaspora"—a people without a fixed place, living in cultural situations that render faith homeless.[40] The very meaning of their faith is rooted in this sense of dislocation, of pursuing faith in a desert that does not support it, and where external signposts are infrequent to nonexistent.

This leads us to explore more deeply the notion of spiritual dislocation. And nowhere do we find this experience more acutely felt than in the throes of suffering.

2

Homelessness in the Face of Suffering

> They say people in hell suffer eternal pain because of the loss of God—they would go through all that suffering if they had just a little hope of possessing God.—In my soul I feel just that terrible pain of loss—of God not wanting me—of God not being God—of God not really existing. . . . In my heart there is no faith. . . . I don't believe.
>
> —Saint Teresa of Calcutta
> *Come Be My Light: The Private Writing of the Saint of Calcutta*

Mother Teresa of Calcutta (Kolkata), recently canonized a saint, forced herself into and also suffered several massive dislocations in her lifetime. Born in 1910 in what is now known as Macedonia, then part of the Ottoman Empire, she was Albanian by ethnicity and culture, and she studied in Ireland before moving to India. Along the way she learned both English and Bengali, undergoing major cultural adjustments in order to serve the poor. She later founded the Missionaries of Charity, living among and serving the dying and destitute in the teeming Indian city. This was searing work, for it pushed her into the heart of a degree of human suffering that she had never before encountered, and which few in the global North ever do encounter. It raised for her deep questions about her faith, and about the God in whom she had placed her life. Perhaps the most severe of her dislocations was not geographic, but spiritual, concerning her sense of God. For in the midst of witnessing so much human suffering, she herself was led into a darkness so impenetrable that she spent years not knowing how to locate God—where God was to be found in the midst of so much pain. She who worked among the uprooted and homeless of the earth had to contend with a spiritual homelessness that was a very real affliction.[1]

There is something almost reassuring about reading her diaries, because they are a reminder that when we ourselves might find God inaccessible, or when we might find ourselves in the throes of the despair of not believing, we are not standing on completely unfamiliar terrain. That road has been trodden before us by the saints. For Teresa of Calcutta herself stands in the company of such spiritual "masters" as John of the Cross, Ignatius of Loyola, and her own namesake, Thérèse de Lisieux.[2] But in Teresa of Calcutta, we find a more recent statement of the darkness of faith: at least for a time, she cannot believe. She knows the temptation of atheism, to find oneself dislocated from the navigation points that once made God seem familiar and accessible, to find oneself "homeless" with regard to the "home" that was once known as God. How is it that this celebrated saint could have known and suffered the temptation to atheism?

This temptation to atheism, born of suffering, may be especially apposite to our age, what the Jewish philosopher Martin Buber, called the epoch of homelessness. This stands in contrast to the previous era, which he termed the epoch of habitation, aligned with an Aristotelian view of a well-ordered and hierarchically structured universe. The epoch of habitation offered a cosmology of "unsurpassable clarity as a universe of *things*" where the human is one of these things and is "an objectively comprehensible species beside other species."[3] In this view the human species has a sense of home, a sense of place in the universe as a whole. In the Aristotelian cosmos, this creaturely habitation occupied a middle place in a cosmic hierarchy. "Man" was the measure of all things and stood at the center of a cosmos rationally ordered around this supremely rational animal. In such a universe, it was easy to situate the human in relation to God, for God presided over the entire structure of things and is its prime mover. With various permutations, this geocentric schema was the presumed picture of the universe, the governing cosmological paradigm, until the great crisis over the claims of Galileo in the seventeenth century.

This model stands in contrast, Buber says, to the epoch of homelessness limned by Aristotle's teacher, Plato, in the *Timaeus*. Here, the human being does not belong to the world of things (air, earth, fire, and water) but is an embodied soul, caught between this earthly imprisonment and the higher aspirations of his pure nature. The human participates in a reality that in some way reflects the eternal form of which the world is an expression as a creation of the Demiurge.[4] This general model, of the human standing between the earth and heaven, finds its way into Augustine's world view, as he confesses to being influenced by "the Platonists" after his immersion in a Manichaean dualism that allowed for such subtlety.[5] Buber's Platonic-Augustinian human being is "homeless in the world, solitary between the higher and the lower powers, [and] he remains homeless and solitary even after he found salvation in Christianity as a redemption that had already taken place."[6] Theologically speaking, this model comports with a pessimistic view of humanity as fatally wounded, cast from a "Paradise Lost" but not without hope, and in virtually eternal search of a salvation from his wanderings.[7] This view aligns as well with the post-Copernican cosmology and with a post-Newtonian physics, both of which would establish a cosmic image of homelessness—of a human existence without fixity. Post-Copernican cosmology would do it by placing the human in a radically eccentric and improbably remote place in the cosmos, and post-Newtonian physics would do it by subjecting the human to the same unpredictable chaos as the rest of the universe. So homelessness becomes at once a physical or cosmic and an existential, even spiritual, reality for humankind.[8]

One constant across both epochs, of habitation and of homelessness, is the reality of physical suffering, pain, decline, and death. Let us consider this form of human suffering in relation to God, understood here for the moment as the omnipotent supreme being commonly assumed in classical theology, Elizabeth Johnson's "God of theism." In the epoch of habitation, physical suffering can be seen as belonging to the natural order established by God, who created all things in freedom, including human beings. According to this view, physical suffering, and the consequences of it, leading up to and including death, are understood to result from God's judgment on the "Sin of Adam." Here, the punishments inflicted by God on Adam and Eve, and their expulsion from the Garden of Eden into a hostile world where they suddenly had to search for a dwelling place for themselves, were the result of a well-deserved yet merciful divine judgment. The whole of human existence, including the suffering endured as a result of natural catastrophe, would thereby be cast in the shadow of this judgment and interpreted as an expression of divine judgment. The Flood story is a vivid illustration of this theology of judgment.[9] In this construction, suffering of any kind is ultimately tied to God's judgment on the human race for the sin of Adam.

It is this condition of suffering, at least partly the result of divine judgment, that God in his mercy meets with a number of redemptive missions, the last of which, according to the Christian narrative, is the sending of his Son. Anselm of Canterbury has asked, "*Cur Deus homo?*" Why did God become human?[10] The answer: In order to save us from ourselves and thus to reestablish the order that was lost—to restore us to our habitation, to a state of undefiled nature, to a sense of being at home in the place God originally placed us in relation to God's Self. The dislocation brought on by the sin of the Garden of Eden leads to the dislocation of God by becoming human, culminating in the agony of Jesus in the Garden of Gethsemane, and his sense of abandonment by God while dying on the cross.[11]

As already mentioned, this story involves a divine move. For the narrative unfolds from the question, "Why did God become human?" And this leads us naturally to the Incarnation. The center of this drama, Jesus, is himself not at home in the world. He is caught between earth and heaven in a painful tension. During his earthly life he literally has no place to lay his head; he is homeless in a very real way. And he suffers, greatly, not only in his spirit, but in his body. The Scriptures suggest that while enduring the agony of the cross he experienced the dereliction of abandonment by God—a sense that God was not there—and that he cried out into what Rahner described as "the trackless dark" and "the wilderness of God."[12] There is no orientation point in the darkness of that night, no Google map out of the wilderness, no ultimate rationality to draw order out of the chaos of suffering, both actual and anticipated.

For all who float in this realm of homelessness, marked by so much suffering, not only are there few if any trustworthy bearings, but the heavens can seem a limitless, lifeless, and merciless void, a great silent space that does not so much as echo back our cries. As Buber writes: "Pascal, the great scientist, a mathematician and a physicist, young and destined to die early, experienced beneath the starry heavens not merely, as Kant did, their majesty, but still more powerfully their uncanniness: *le silence eternal de ces espace infini m'effraie*" (the eternal silence of that infinite space stirs fear within me).[13] As Buber observes, Pascal expresses here "the sobriety of the man who has become more deeply solitary than ever before, and with a sober pathos he frames the anthropological question afresh: *qu'est ce qu'un homme dan l'infini?*" (what is a human being in the midst of the infinite?).[14] In this epoch of homelessness, the human being is alone in his or her suffering, because God no longer seems to be connected with the human creature. God, seems unmoored from the earth, distant from the suffering of humankind, indeed from all the groaning of creation (Rom 8:19). And so the temptation toward some form of atheism, of an inability to affirm that God exists, is plausible. "*In my soul I feel just that terrible pain of loss—of God not wanting me—of God not being God—of God not really existing. . . . In my heart there is no faith. . . . I don't believe.*" Yet simultaneously, we insist, a God must have something to do with this whole process, which, according to Newton's belief, God set in motion in the first place.

* * *

This takes us to the heart of the problem of locating God. What fundamentally unsettled Mother Teresa was not some philosophical doubt. It was, rather the insuperable reality of suffering. This, even more than a shift in cosmological outlook, is what has led to so much existential and spiritual dislocation. How then are we to locate God with respect to human suffering? The framing of the problem takes us back to the 1755 Lisbon earthquake, a catastrophe of such monumental proportions that it gave rise to new and trenchant questions about how we can maintain faith in God. In his *Theodicy* (1710), Gottfried Leibniz asked how we can square the suffering that befalls us with an all-good and all-powerful God. The seeming comfort of Leibniz's conclusion, that we live in "the best of all possible worlds," was unsettled by the event of 1755—a time, we should remember, when human beings could no longer imagine that they were situated at the center of the cosmos; the Galileo affair, a dispute over cosmology and the natural philosophy that sustained it, had occurred one hundred years earlier. A paradigm shift was already well under way.[15] So the theodicy question moved beyond questions of cosmology (habitation vs. homelessness) to a consideration of God. What kind of God are we imagining here for faith?

In his book *Evil and the God of Love*, John Hick somewhat anachronistically applies the term "theodicy" to thinkers such as Irenaeus and Augustine, for whom the very idea of needing to establish a philosophical justification of God in the face of the problem of evil would have been unimaginable.[16] For Augustine in particular the question was rather how one could place the suffering consequent upon sin within the schema of an all-provident and all-knowing God. This question differs from the theodicy question as Leibniz framed it because it introduces into the discussion something that had been largely abstracted from later theories of theodicy: moral evil, and the tangled relationships between free will and divine foreknowledge. The issue for Augustine was that foreknowledge implied necessity, and therefore it would seem that God, by dint of his foreknowledge, somehow was the cause of evil.[17] But Augustine also wanted to safeguard the claim that human beings are endowed with free will. Augustine worked at this problem in several writings throughout his career, and endeavored to show that despite divine foreknowledge, the free will of human beings remained intact.[18] In this approach, God would have to justify God's very Self only if human beings had nothing to do with their own suffering, as in the case of natural catastrophes that mercilessly inflict both suffering and death on vast stretches of living things. But in Augustine's world, things are different. Influenced by Paul (e.g., Rom 8:20–22), but also by his early Manichaeism, it was not difficult for Augustine to see creation itself infected by human sinfulness and divine judgment upon that sinfulness; he sees signs of it even in the squalling of babies for mother's milk.[19] Augustine saw the chaos that marks nature as in some way the consequence of sin. Thomas Aquinas would follow Augustine in this view, but would take a somewhat less deterministic view of the relationship between free will and divine providence. His discussion of divine knowledge, providence, and predestination in the *Summa Theologiae* presents a highly refined and nuanced doctrine of predestination that safeguarded human freedom and autonomy. Yes, the divine mind of God knows all that has occurred or will occur, for the divine mind holds everything in an eternal present that transcends time. Therefore, the divine knowledge is a knowledge of contingencies as well as of the execution and outcomes of free acts of will. There is held in tension, therefore, the absolute transcendence of God who beholds all, and the freedom and autonomy of the creature. What is "necessary" in the eternal present of the divine mind remains contingent within the continuum of space and time that we humans inhabit.[20]

But these ancient discourses on providence were to be displaced by a philosophical theodicy. The shortcomings of that theodicy project have been noted by several scholars, such as theologians John Thiel and Terrence Tilley, who argue that theodicy only served to further distance God from human action, and that these philosophical projects do not sufficiently take into account the data of revelation on which faith in God depends.[21] Although these theological critiques of theodicy are to my mind valid, the deeper problem with theodicy is that it presumes a God who has been cast in question in the epoch of homelessness: For not only has post-Newtonian physics unmoored the old God from the earth and the cosmos; so, too, the notion of an expanding universe in continuing evolution has made it ever more difficult to imagine how to locate the divine action of God to an autonomous cosmos. In an expanding picture of the universe, an ever more rapid movement outward strains our categories of the finite, traditionally tied to a space-time continuum, into a virtually infinite calculus. We cannot speak with confidence of a contained universe, or of a universe with boundaries, outside of which, according to the old model, God would somehow be standing, encompassing the whole. For this would be to reduce God, in actuality, to another layer of reality.[22]

What the evolutionary or expanding universe does with God is far more radical: it restores to God his absolute otherness. God's absolute otherness is not the same thing as God's absolute distance. Yes, God is unmoored, but that is simply to say that God falls outside the rules of this world, and that the laws of nature cannot explain God, much less comprehend God—a fallacy often made when people misunderstand what is meant by natural law, framing it in terms of a static understanding of nature.[23] But the very fact that God falls outside the laws of nature raises further problems with regard to suffering—a recasting of the old problems. For now we have to ask whether God is somehow responsible for the blind and random forces of nature that, in an evolutionary march, result in so much suffering and death. We are in a sense back to the theodicy question, but in a new key: Why is it that this God, now untethered from the universe, nevertheless has set things up so that the only way forward is through suffering and death? Does this mean that somehow God has intended these things in the first place? And if so, what does that imply about God?

There are two broad ways of approaching this problem. One is to grant nature its autonomy, an autonomy that does not depend on a God. In that autonomy, part of the "goodness" of nature, following its own autonomous course, is the suffering that we experience as the pawns of nature, tossed about like so much flotsam and jetsam. This suffering is something which, to some degree, we must simply accept, just as we accept the tides, winds, and movement of the stars. Death, too, is a natural phenomenon, a datum of reality. Although this view has a certain Stoic appeal, it too readily leads toward a sense of fate, meaninglessness, and, ultimately, even nihilism.

However, if we wish to save God, this view can lead to a view of God that suits our current purposes. Charles Taylor speaks of the rise of a "Providential Deism" that led, he argues, to an "exclusive humanism" that follows on disenchantment, and "the sense that God is an indispensable source for our spiritual and moral life." But the result is that God is reduced to a "power" or force, and religion becomes reduced to ethics, "carrying out God's goals (= our goals) in the world."[24] Such a position does not mark an advance on the road toward a recovery of belief in the God of Abram, Isaac, and Jacob. Yet it might help bolster faith in a weakened God of theism.

In a second approach, we could opt for the autonomous creation, but at the same time reconsider what we mean by divine action in relation to creation. This implies that older models of providence, with their Christian provenance in Paul, Augustine, Boethius, and Aquinas (but harking back to Plato, the Neoplatonists, and Cicero) and leading up to the debates of theodicy, need to be interrogated anew, perhaps leading to a different understanding of divine providence. I would endorse here, as such an alternate route, one that came out of the early modern humanism of the University of Paris, where one student in the early sixteenth century was Ignatius of Loyola.[25] The historical scholarship of Hugo Rahner has recast Ignatius as a theologian in his own right, although not of the systematic kind.[26] His was a sapiential theology that emerged from his experiences of a God who was as yet still moored to the cosmos, and yet the author of an infinite universe. For Ignatius, the providence of God was not a map for navigating the shoals of life, and the central issue was not divine foreknowledge as in any way determining freedom. Rather, it was the relationship between creaturely freedom and God's self-giving love, God's grace. The providence of God was seen as an activity, ongoing and unceasing, corresponding to God's being—a being not standing outside the pageant of creation, but a being-in-unceasing-activity within the present moment. Pure act, ever self-giving. This is a God of time even more than a God of place—a God of the eternality of the moment, and of moments cascading one upon the other. God works in concert with creaturely freedom but does not predetermine free acts or events of nature. Human beings and creatures maintain their creaturely autonomy. We get a glimpse of this theology in the final phase of the Spiritual Exercises, the Contemplation to Attain Divine Love:

> I will consider how God labors and works for me in all the creatures on the face of the earth; . . . working in the heavens, elements, plants, fruits, cattle, and all the rest—giving them their existence, conserving them, concurring with their vegetative and sensitive activities, and so forth. . . . I will consider how all good things and gifts descend from above . . . just as the rays come down from the sun, or the rains from their source.[27]

God is not featured as the Uncaused Cause, but rather as Love, whose being *is* creating act, and who, by virtue of God's being, establishes creation— that which is not God—in its full autonomy and freedom. It resolves the problem of divine foreknowledge by removing it from a rigid causative framework, and by claiming only the "necessity" of the present moment, which is held in the view of a loving divine mind and heart. It seems to me that this model of providence is more apposite to our quantum and evolutionary-charged imaginations than are the static notions of God's providence that were presumed by many in the past. God remains dislocated, decentered from a cosmological perspective, but not for that reason disengaged or absent from reality.[28]

But, for the suffering, for the grieving of this world, where does this lead us? What does it mean to believe in such an unmoored but not disengaged God? In the midst of earthly despair, what reason is there not to commit suicide and bring an end to what seems meaningless? Why indeed believe if life seems to offer no more than a trial of endurance? In the face of such questions Rahner struggles to maintain strict intellectual honesty in the face of all that we are dealing with here: the sheer fact of suffering and death, the loss of a former sense of habitation due to our being situated in a vast and expanding universe, the unfathomable elusiveness of any location of God, and the microcosm that is the human being—an intersection of matter and spirit. Rahner is clear in stating that there is no escaping the harshness of suffering and the unanswerable finality of death.[29] These are inalienable aspects of creation that we, in our creatureliness, are fated to undergo—just as did Jesus Christ, whose appearance occurs within the evolution of the cosmos, not as an extrinsic insertion into it.[30] Because Jesus Christ was fully human and both suffered and died, the Christian cannot look on faith as an opiate or an analgesic.[31] Certain forms of religion may well serve as palliatives for some, but faith in Jesus Christ does not permit an escape from suffering or a denial of its force in our lives. For the pain of suffering lies at the heart of the revelation of who God is for the creature.

To carry this further, there is a convergence of the mystery of suffering with the mystery of God: the incomprehensibility of suffering is, because of Jesus's foundational experience, part of the revelation of the incomprehensibility of God—not of God God's Self, but of God's incomprehensibility:

> The incomprehensibility of suffering is part of the incomprehensibility of God. Not in the sense that we could deduce it as necessary and thus inevitably as clarified from something else that we already know of God. If this were so it would not be at all incomprehensible. But the very fact that it is really and eternally incomprehensible means that suffering is truly a manifestation of God's incomprehensibility in his nature and in God's freedom.[32]

This sentence is pregnant with meaning and various presuppositions that Rahner lays out earlier in his essay, but one key insight is that we cannot, in theodicy-like fashion, calculate divine action or gauge divine freedom in some a priori fashion.

So what, then, of evil? Evil is not necessarily the unfathomable mystery we always make it out to be. We can begin to understanding it as parasitic of the good, that it presupposes the good. This does not mean that evil is not real, but that its existence depends on the prior good of things as they have been and are being created. And God, who is working on and sustaining all things in love, as Ignatius would have it, is drawing forth what is good, even from death. Neither evil nor death in themselves have anything to do with God in God's Self.[33] But this divine acting in love is what the raising of Jesus from the dead reveals and what constitutes the dawn of Christian faith itself.

Rahner by no means wishes to suggest that therefore all is settled and that God has finally been captured again and that we can return to our habitations of old. It is an ever "new creation" that is under way through the divine action. This means that Christians will be both utter realists about creaturely life as we in fact experience it and, at the same time, because of what has been disclosed by God of God's Self already, beings of self-transcending hope. This hope need not lead to an unrealistic optimism, a naïve utopianism, but rather to the living of the divinely endowed (theological) virtue of hope, understood as a mode of being-in-act, a living into and for the "future" in God. Believing, then, is not in the first instance the giving of intellectual assent to formulations of faith, but an act of bearing being on the part of the suffering creature, a *kenosis* unto a God who cannot be located in the beyond, yet who by virtue of the divine nature is acting upon the suffering of the cosmos in love, annihilating the power of parasitic evil and generating the good of a new creation.

Finally, Rahner can say that yes, God is far from us, especially if we ask where God lies within the experience of creaturehood in an epoch of homelessness. Indeed, a sense that God is unmoored and distant can lead to despair. But it is simply despair in the ability to believe any longer a false notion of God, an intellectual or even religious idol. That would be the God who was so at issue in the heyday of theodicy, but also the God who has been presupposed in much of the debates between religion and science, a version of the God of theism. This omnipotent, omniscient supernatural being, a being among beings, is, in the final analysis, another problematic object.[34] Such objective constructions of God are delimiting, misleading, and false. For the God we are concerned with is unmoored from the world of theological round and square holes, indeed from the world or laws of nature. At the same time, with an Augustinian insight that we occasionally find in Rahner, this God is nearer to us than we are to ourselves—*intimior intimo meo*.[35] Yet this God does not displace our freedom, does not steer our course, and is not the cause of our suffering or death. As a positively theological statement we can say that this is a God revealed in an emphatic *No!* to suffering and death in the resurrection of Jesus from the dead, and an emphatic *Yes!* in the good of creation.[36] It is not the mystery of evil that should preoccupy us; it is the mystery of God that is so much denser. "When we speak of God we do not clear up a puzzle; we draw attention to a mystery."[37] This is the mystery with which we must live, in life, in faith, in prayer, as we suffer through this existence and eventually die. But as we gaze at the stars, which Ignatius did through tears, and as Pascal did in fear and loneliness, we have ample warrant to give ourselves over to this unfathomable Mystery in peace, partly because of the Christian conviction that this elusive God has entered into our own state of homelessness, and remains the pioneer of our pilgrimage of faith.

3

The Dislocation of the Divine Kenosis

> For while all things were in quiet silence, and the night was in the midst of her course, Thy almighty word leapt down from heaven from thy royal throne, as a fierce conqueror into the midst of the land of destruction.
>
> —Wisdom 18:11

If God can seem to be distant and removed from the dislocations of human suffering, the Christian story recalls that God has voluntarily undertaken a divine dislocation, captured in the Christian doctrine of the Incarnation of the Son. This claim, that the unchanging, absolutely transcendent and infinite God would *choose* to *become* present in creation in the form of a finite creature—is assuredly one of the boldest claims about God ever to have been made among the three major monotheistic religions of the West. Here we move from the realm of questions and theories about how God can be said to be involved in creation—not God's responsibility for so much evil and suffering—but what God does about it. We return to Anselm's question, "Why did God become human?" Karl Rahner suggested that we can imagine that the Incarnation seems to be a massive disruption in the created order of things or a working of God into his creation in the course of its evolution. Either way, the implication will be that God, in and through one of the triune persons, the Son, has left the heavenly realms, and that idea by itself dramatically challenges any understanding of God as eternally unchanging and the occupant of an empyrean realm. For in this picture, God has willed to become unmoored from the heavens in order to become inserted into a human world of existential upheaval, a world that sin has distorted—what the book of Wisdom calls "the land of destruction." In the Gospel of John, this divine self-dislocation is personified as the descent and incarnation of the Logos, or Word: God's self-utterance. This Logos moves into the flesh, and becomes human. "He pitched his tent among us" (Jn 1:14). The Incarnation is the result of a divine movement into the transitoriness and the contingency of the human estate, found on this lonely outer edge of creation.

Let us turn here again to Ignatius of Loyola. This incarnational view represents the religious imaginary landscape in which he was steeped. Although Ignatius certainly recognized that the path to God is charted through the human, and through the natural world in general, he was also deeply aware of a fundamental moral fissure in this world, and saw the plain marks of sin and darkness within it. Life here on earth involves a conflict, a *lucha*, between the power of sin over our freedom and our desire to exercise that freedom in a way that responds to the love that God has so manifestly shown us.[1] But we need help in this struggle, and that help comes through the divine movement of the Incarnation. Hugo Rahner describes the Incarnation as a divine movement occurring "between earth and heaven."[2] He emphasizes the importance in Ignatius's view of the world of the notion of the divine descent from above (*de arriba*), much as we find a descent of the Word marked in the prologue of the Gospel of John. The source and goal of all created reality is "from above" and "the essential note of Ignatian theology is the way of descent."[3] This divine descent, which we also see inscribed in the Christological hymn of Philippians 2, deeply imbues the Ignatian imagination, and is especially evident in the contemplation on the Incarnation in the Spiritual Exercises.

In this contemplation, Ignatius paints a truly charming picture of the divine *kenosis*. The divine persons peer from the edge of the heavens, gazing on the life of human beings down below:

"Here, it is how the three divine persons looked at all the plain or circuit of all the world, full of people, and how, seeing that all were going down to hell, they decide in their eternity, that the Second Person should become a human being, in order to save the human race."[4]

The divine persons see that the human race is in a perilous state, disoriented by sin and self-delusion ("going down to hell"). Like God's love itself, the initiative of a movement between earth and heaven begins entirely with God (cf. 1 Jn 4:10), who resides above, *de arriba*. Then Ignatius focuses on the interplay between the divine persons and human beings on earth: hearing what the people of the earth are saying, what the divine persons are saying among themselves, and what the people of the earth are doing, what the divine persons are doing, "that is, bringing about the most holy Incarnation."[5] All of this is done with a view toward the conclusion of the contemplation, beseeching the Trinity, the eternal Word incarnate, and Mary "according to what I perceive in my heart, that I may better follow and imitate Our Lord, who in this way has recently become a human being."[6]

Hugo Rahner describes what is happening in this kind of movement of the religious imagination:

> This Ignatian theology of Christ effects a sort of "reduction" of "above" to "below," by way of the divine Majesty put to death on the cross. . . . The royal throne of the Father is confronted by "the face and circumference of the earth" [*SpExx* 102, 103], and below this again is the utmost abyss beyond which no further descent is possible: the hell into which [people] must "descend" [*SpExx* 102], though they are able to rise again from it in the Mediator to the glory of the Father, because the Word—as the radiant source—had himself "come down from above" [*SpExx* 237] and is thus "at the feet of the most Holy Trinity," where he "implores the Trinity for forgiveness." In Christ, then, the "above" of the Father has become permanently fused into the elements and atoms of the world "below." The dialogue on the royal throne ends in the room at Nazareth.[7]

This is a picture of great motion, an event, hardly of a static state of affairs. The Incarnation becomes a way of speaking about the lengths to which God will go in order to meet the human beings in their own states of dislocation. The only way for God to meet humankind is to move to where they are, and to participate in and become part of the human condition. But as Johannes Metz has expressed so memorably, this very feat is itself an act of the greatest relinquishment, of God's becoming poor.[8]

The divine dislocation implied in John and made explicit in Ignatius is first imagined in the primitive Christological hymn quoted in Paul's Letter to the Philippians (2:1–11), mentioned earlier. Paul's letter is an exhortation that uses the divine descent as an example of the kind of self-disposing interior motion that belonged to Jesus,

> who, though he was in the form of God
> did not regard equality with God as something to be exploited
> but emptied himself
> taking the form of a slave,
> being born in human likeness.
> And being found in human form,
> he humbled himself
> and became obedient to the point of death—
> even death on a cross.

The dislocation continues, to his being raised and, as it were, ensconced again in the heavenly places, now given a divine dignity as bearer of the holy name of God (Lord) that was first cryptically imparted at Sinai:

> Therefore, God also highly exalted him
> and gave him the name
> that is above every name,
> so that at the name of Jesus
> every knee should bend,
> in heaven and on earth and under the earth,
> and every tongue should confess
> that Jesus Christ is Lord,
> to the glory of God the Father.

God, in the divine person of the Son, becomes unmoored and empties himself into and as human flesh in the person of Jesus Christ and in the form of a slave.

This hymn does not bear the theological precision of later church pronouncements on the Incarnation offered by the early councils of the church, which were born of much theological controversy. For example, Philippians refers not to human or divine natures (*physei*), as later church councils would, but uses the less philosophically precise language of "forms" (*morphei*), both divine and human. The Son, who was in the form of the divine, now takes on the form of the human. And the particularities of that human form are dramatic, as if to underscore the radical statement that is being made: he submits to the status of a slave (*doulos*), a human being with no standing as a person—a nonperson in the ancient world, and indeed in any age, including our own. This absolute dislocation of the divinity reveals that God desires to enter into solidarity with the lowest of human beings—those who are rejected or, even worse, whose very existence is ignored, denied, or expunged. In the dominant Christian narrative, as enshrined by the Nicene Creed, this "coming down from heaven" occurs "for us and for our salvation," for, according to the tradition from Paul through Anselm and beyond, all are deemed sinners in need of salvation. The Philippians hymn declares that that salvation for all takes place in and through the suffering and ignominious death of the most rejected of human beings, and that the lowest of human estates is where God desires to be located and found.[9] This nadir of history is the apogee of the divine dislocation, for it is also the disclosure of precisely where God has come to dwell within the lot of the human—in the humiliation, suffering, and death of the slave who is executed as a state criminal. This is a dramatic dislocation indeed. Yet this death would also reveal something more: the omnipresence and ultimate omnipotence of God's powerful love (Rom 8:35–39), spread throughout the universe to all humankind and to every creature, that all might be reconciled and saved (Col 1:15–20; 1 Tm 2:4). The greatest imaginable creaturely weakness discloses the absolute gift of greatest magnitude. The way that God's love is shown becomes a challenge to human wisdom (cf. 1 Cor 1:25).

* * *

In his classic book *Poverty of Spirit* Metz offers the outlines of such a theological understanding of the divine *kenosis*, one that serves as a pattern for those who would count themselves among believers. Metz rests his argument on the foundation of Philippians 2, but also on the church's further reflection as reflected in the doctrinal developments of the writings of the fathers and the early church councils. Metz presumes the accomplishment of the Council of Chalcedon (451). That council, called by Pope Leo I (the Great), was concerned with the teaching among some that if Jesus was divine, which was confirmed by the Council of Nicea (325) when it said the he was of the same substance (*homoousios*) as the Father, then he could not also have been authentically and truly human. A number of theologians expressed some form of this idea, generally gathered under the title of docetism and monophysitism. Docetists taught that Jesus only *seemed* to be human, but was in fact only divine. The humanity was a kind of costume for the divinity. Monophysites taught that the divine nature not only governed the human, but replaced it when the two natures met; thus Jesus was composed of only one, divine, nature. From either approach, Jesus was clearly not fully human and was situated so far above and beyond the normal state of human beings as to be inaccessible. Refuting such views, Chalcedon held that the two natures, united in the person of the Word or Son of God, each enjoyed a full integrity, working in harmony with each other and in a single divine saving work (for us and our salvation).[10] Pope Leo had expressed this doctrine earlier, in a letter to Flavian, the bishop of Constantinople:

> The character proper to each of the two natures which come together in one person being therefore preserved, lowliness was taken on by majesty, weakness by strength, mortality by eternity. And, in order to pay the debt of our condition, the inviolable nature was united to a nature open to suffering so that, as was fitting to heal our wounds, one and the same "mediator between God and humankind, the man Christ Jesus" (1 Tm 2:5) could die in one nature and not in the other. The true God, therefore, was born with the complete

> and perfect nature of a true man; he is complete in his own properties and complete in ours.[11]

Jesus, the incarnate Son, was not only one in being with the Father but also one in being with humanity, possessing a full and uncompromised human nature. The key passage from Chalcedon reads:

> Following, therefore, the holy Fathers, we unanimously teach to confess one and the same Son, our Lord Jesus Christ, the same perfect in divinity and perfect in humanity, the same truly God and truly man composed of rational soul and body, the same one in being (*homoousios*) with the Father as to the divinity and one in being (*homoousios*) with us as to the humanity, like unto us in all things but sin.[12]

The architect of the council, Pope Leo, had delivered a sermon on Christmas that captured beautifully not only what was to become the central insight of Chalcedon's teaching but also something more: that not only had God entered fully into the realm of the human, but, as a result, the human had been given a share in the divine nature:

> And so, dearly beloved, let us give thanks to God the Father through his Son in the Holy Spirit. In his great and merciful love for us he has taken pity on us, and when we were dead in sin he has brought us to life along with Christ, that we might be in him a new creation a new work of his fashioning. And so away with the old man and his deeds. Having attained a share in the birth of Christ, let us renounce the works of the flesh. O Christian, realize your nobility! Now that you have been given a share in the divine nature, do not ignobly return to your old meanness.[13]

This idea, that by virtue of the Incarnation, human beings have been given a share in the divine, was echoed by Pope John Paul II in his inaugural encyclical, *Redemptor Hominis*, published in 1979, where he leaned heavily on the teaching of the Pastoral Constitution of the Church in the Modern World (*Gaudium et Spes*), one of the key documents from the Second Vatican Council (1962–65):

> Human nature, by the very fact that it was assumed, not absorbed, in him, has been raised in us also to a dignity beyond compare.[14] For, by his incarnation, he, the son of God, in a certain way united himself with each human person. He worked with human hands, he thought with a human mind. He acted with a human will, and with a human heart he loved. Born of the Virgin Mary, he has truly been made one of us, "like to us in all things except sin," he, the Redeemer of humankind.[15]

There is very strong foundation, then, for understanding the Incarnation as the event in which God moves outside God's Self, the Infinite becoming finite, the Eternal coming to be in time.[16]

All of this is background to the theology of Jesus as the Christ that unfolds in Metz's *Poverty of Spirit*. Metz begins his reflections on the poverty of Christ by focusing on the temptation of Jesus in the desert (Mt 4:1–11; Lk 4:1–13). These passages are often interpreted as literal or figurative representations of Jesus's internal spiritual struggle over his future, the outcome of which struggle was the inauguration of his ministry. Metz reads these passages differently, as representing the temptation of Christ to resist participation in the *kenosis*, the divine self-dislocation, of which he was the expression: to resist the self-renunciation of becoming poor that lay at the heart of God's becoming human. "[Satan] wants God to remain distant and unreachable." But, as Metz beautifully expresses it:

> Instead, Jesus subjected himself to our plight. He immersed himself in our misery and followed our road to the end. He did not escape from the torment of our life, nobly repudiating humanity. With the full weight of his divinity he descended into the abyss of human existence, penetrating its darkest depths. He was not spared from the dark mystery of our poverty as human beings.[17]

Metz is describing a divine movement into the dregs, the poverty, of human existence. One key implication of this poverty of the human spirit is that we do not own ourselves: our very being is sheer gift, the emergence in space and time of what God in the divine largesse has brought into being for no reason other than love. We are radically dependent on this divine largesse, and at the same time, are utterly free because of it. Elaborating on this idea, theologian Kathryn Tanner speaks of the "non-competitive relation" between human beings and God. "The creature's receiving from God does not then require its passivity in the world: God's activity as the giver of ourselves need not come at the expense of our own activity. Instead, the creature receives from God its very activity as a good."[18] Christian faith claims this to be true because it was revealed in Jesus, who was the one in whom dislocation of God met humanity in its own dislocation of sinfulness and existential homelessness. And Jesus executed his mission in complete freedom and autonomy. For freedom is the openness of human spirit toward the God who bestows the gift of creaturely autonomy out of love. The divine love is perfect because it is not at all possessive, but is rather dispossessive, desiring the complete freedom of the beloved. However, as creatures living in space and time, and precisely as persons, this freedom is given and filtered through relations with others. It is in and through their relations with others that human beings express their freedom of spirit, which is also a movement toward God. So in loving the other, the neighbor, as ourselves, we are loving God.

> Poverty of spirit does not bring us from human beings to God by isolating these components into separate little packages: God-Me-Others. . . . It operates through the radical depths of human encounter itself. In total self-abandonment and full commitment to another we become completely poor, and the depths of infinite mystery open up to us from within this other person.[19]

We can witness the validity of this statement in so many ways, especially in what Catholic theologian and ethicist James Keenan has called "entering the chaos of the world."[20] We cannot enter into another's chaos unless we have a profound sense of our own chaos, of our own need to be met by others there—of our poverty. There is a strength in knowing our own poverty, our own need, which creates the condition of possibility for being there for others.

It is this kind of self-knowledge that has inspired the most beloved of the saints, canonized or not, whose sheer humanity, the very poverty of it, proved a balm for others. One in whom all of this came together—the poverty of self, the poverty of Christ, and the poverty of others—was Saint Francis, whose very personal presence brought healing because of the poverty of Christ people found in him—Christ who had humbled himself to meet them in their own poverty. Francis possessed a profound mystical grasp of the Incarnation and of God's humbling meeting of humanity in one of us, an insight that has been captured by Paul: "For you know the grace of our Lord Jesus Christ, that though he was rich, yet for your sake he became poor, so that you through his poverty might become rich" (2 Cor 8:9). This inspiration has radiated in and through the lives of many other holy men and women.

In the Incarnation, therefore, we have the convergence of three moments of dislocation: First, there is the dislocation found in the *kenosis* of God in Jesus, where God moves outside God's Self in a motion of love "for us and for our salvation." This we see reflected in the imagery of the Ignatian contemplation on the Incarnation. It is a divine initiative, for God "first loved us" (1 Jn 4:19). Second, that divine dislocation, that kenotic love, meets the ontological dislocation of the human condition (the human condition set awry by a history of sin) and the existential dislocations of the human condition (that chaos brought about by sin and consequent suffering). That meeting, between the divine and the human, establishes a dwelling place, a meeting point, where the human can find an orientation and hope for fulfillment, a home despite all dislocations, in God. There God enters fully into the dislocated human condition, and suffers and dies in full solidarity with human beings. Third, human beings, now located by and joined with God in Jesus Christ, are moved by the Spirit to enter freely into a new stage of dislocation, in history, to go forth from that home of union with God into the world of other human beings who find themselves dislocated, to enter into and carry on the mission of the Reign of God. Here we are speaking of a recovery of belief, not simply as a matter of the retrieval of doctrine about Christ and the things of God, but as living the mystery of God in Christ, entering into what Karl Rahner called a "mystagogy" of faith, to which I shall turn in the epilogue of this book.

4

The Dislocation of Solidarity with the Crucified

> Today I have come to gather up this church and convent that has been profaned, this tabernacle that has been destroyed and above all else to gather up this people that has been humiliated and unnecessarily sacrificed. . . . You are an image of the wronged Divinity that is spoken about in the first reading in prophetic and mysterious language—language that represents Christ nailed to the cross and pierced by a lance. You are the image of all people, who like yourselves, have been pierced and abused. But if you suffer this pain with faith, then you will give your suffering a redemptive meaning and the people of Aguilares will sing a joyful hymn of liberation.
>
> —Blessed Oscar Romero, bishop and martyr,
> Sermon at Church in Aguilares

I referred in the last chapter to the "Contemplation to Attain Love," the conclusion of the *Spiritual Exercises of St. Ignatius*. It is a beautiful image of God's descent: a way of imagining the divine dislocation that eventuates in the Incarnation and of God's entering into the chaos of the human condition. Yet there is a part of this contemplation that we can easily overlook, where Ignatius says that "love ought to manifest itself in deeds rather than in words."[1] From an ecclesial standpoint, one of the principal modes of believing, alongside liturgy, prayer, doctrine, and institutional practices, is the praxis of the message, that is, living the Gospel message—embodying the Gospel not only by saying it but by doing it. But this emphasis on "doing" the word (or the Law or the Gospel) in fact predates the Gospel and has its roots in the Hebrew Scriptures: "For this command which I enjoin on you today is not too mysterious or remote for you. . . . No, it is something very near to you already in your mouths, and in your hearts; you have only to carry it out" (Dt 30:11–14).

Reality beckons us from any notion of contemplation that would remove us from the world, and draws us into itself, into the world.[2] For there is a dark side to life, a side that can block out the streams of love of which Ignatius speaks, the shadows that contribute to the ongoing struggle to keep believing nimble.[3] I am speaking of the dislocations of suffering and death that make life, and believing, so difficult—the disruptions of life, those events or phenomena that pull us to a halt and suddenly reorder everything: tragedies, such as horrendous acts of violence, terrorism, the inversion of human patterns of habitation and sustenance being brought about by climate change, genocide, the dramatic deleterious effects of hunger, and other disasters. As noted in the introduction, there is perhaps no instance of dislocation more palpable, more dramatic, than that of those people who have literally been uprooted from their lands and homes, and who are caught up in massive upheavals of migration on a scale not seen before in human history. These migrations have been forced by war, terrorism, social and economic upheavals, and, increasingly, natural disasters and climate change. And the fate of migrants and refugees has become a flashpoint for xenophobic politics worldwide. The fate of these suffering people calls us to a degree of solidarity that was almost unimaginable before the world became so interconnected and when interface and encounter among peoples from vastly different places was rare or nonexistent. Yet responding in solidarity lies at the heart of the mission of the Gospel; it increasingly drives to the heart of the church's life, as Pope Francis has tried to impress on the church and the world, starting with his first trip outside Rome, to the island of Lampedusa, where so many refugees from Syria have landed, and where many have perished. Jon Sobrino, a

Spanish-born Jesuit theologian, calls such suffering human beings the crucified peoples.[4]

Who are these crucified peoples? First, there are those who suffer from the kind of poverty that leads to death, the suffering that comes from deprivation of the basic assets of culture because of poverty, disease, war, and natural catastrophe or human-made catastrophes of nature. Second, there is the suffering and death caused by unjust social and economic structures, imposed by "powers" that dominate the poor and weak. The poor and deprived are caught in cycles from which they cannot escape. We see this throughout the world in new forms of slavery, especially sexual slavery, but also in grinding poverty locked in place by castes of color and class. Third, there is the theological-religious reality of such suffering, that the very human beings who do so suffer are the suffering body of Christ in history.[5] The sufferings of these peoples, not only in Central America, but throughout the world, and especially where people are subjected to historical catastrophe caused by other human beings, are the "new name for Golgotha today and their peoples are the Suffering Servant."[6] The crucified peoples are the truly dislocated.

Sobrino describes vividly how a massive Salvadoran earthquake unveiled realities that had otherwise lain hidden behind quaint village façades: as the skin of buildings fell away, the ugliness of poverty, and the massive inequities between the very poor and the rich were laid bare for all to see.[7] This for Sobrino was more than a tragedy; it was a call to action and to fundamental transformation of society.[8] We must look beyond the familiar and enter into solidarity with the crucified peoples of the world if we are to find the true God. These disruptive events, and the dislocations that result from them, compel us to the truth that love "ought to express itself in deeds rather than mere words," an insight of Ignatius that is rooted in the Gospels. The fundamental realities that define everything, including what is the church and where we will find God, are the disruptive realities of human existence that force us to strip away illusions and to confront reality as it is. And this means that a disciple of Jesus cannot evade confronting the frightening entanglements of human suffering.[9]

In El Salvador alone, such suffering led to over 70,000 deaths during a civil war that resulted in massacres and random murders, as well as the uprooting and dislocation of approximately 1 million people (about 20 percent of the entire population),[10] violations of persons and of their human rights, and a legacy of violence and social chaos that endures to this day. This magnitude of suffering is being played out in many other theaters of warfare and violence in our own time, around the globe, most recently in Syria, but also in East Africa and other parts of the globe, in what Pope Francis has called a virtual World War III.[11]

Although Sobrino is certainly interested in the serious questions of theodicy (see chapter 2), his fundamental question is not concerned with how a good and all-powerful God could permit so much suffering. His question is a different one, and could be formulated this way: Why is it that the poor suffer so disproportionately? And, consequently, what does the answer to this question demand of us? The aim of his theological reflections on such suffering is not only to understand it but also to unmask it and eradicate its causes. Unlike theodicy, which puts God in the docket, Sobrino puts human beings in the docket. Rather than explore *theo*dicy, he is concerned with *anthropo*dicy: How can we possibly justify human action, or inaction, that leads to the sins of injustice? He proceeds to demonstrate how even a natural disaster, such as the devastating earthquake that hit El Salvador, serves to unmask the underlying structures of social and economic injustice because the poor are caught up in a physical embodiment of the oppression that marks their lives all along, robbed of land and now without a roof, literally clinging to cliffsides, and suffering death in direct proportion to their poverty, while the rich escape unscathed. The earthquake therefore becomes a summons to undo the unjust structures whose raw framework is exposed by natural disaster. This is true of almost every earthquake that devastates poor countries. Consider Haiti, which has repeatedly been hit by natural disasters and waves of disease that unmask the cruel disparities between the haves and have-nots in the Western hemisphere. The crucified peoples suffer, not only directly by virtue of political, economic, and social oppression, and from the forces of commercial empire and market globalization, but also indirectly through the effects of these powers of distortion on their lives. They are not only impoverished but also disproportionately vulnerable to tragic dislocation and forced migration.

The rather lengthy quotation from the encyclical *Laudato Si'* by Pope Francis powerfully expresses this disproportionate suffering of the poor, here in relation to the effects of climate change:

> Climate change is a global problem with grave implications: environmental, social, economic, political and for the distribution of goods. It represents one of the principal challenges facing humanity in our day. Its worst impact will probably be felt by developing countries in coming decades. Many of the poor live in areas particularly affected by phenomena related to warming, and their means of subsistence are largely dependent on natural reserves and ecosystemic services such as agriculture, fishing and forestry. They have no other financial activities or resources which can enable them to adapt to climate change or to face natural disasters, and their access to social services and protection is very limited. For example, changes in climate, to which animals and plants cannot adapt, lead them to migrate; this in turn affects the livelihood of the poor, who are then forced to leave their homes, with great uncertainty for their future and that of their children. There has been a tragic rise in the number of migrants seeking to flee from the growing poverty caused by environmental degradation. They are not recognized by international conventions as refugees; they bear the loss of the lives they have left behind, without enjoying any legal protection whatsoever. Sadly, there is widespread indifference to such suffering, which is even now taking place throughout our world. Our lack of response to these tragedies involving our brothers and sisters points to the loss of that sense of responsibility for our fellow men and women upon which all civil society is founded.[12]

It seems that the lives of the most vulnerable are of no significance whatsoever, and indeed to some worldly powers, this is indeed the case. If we move this scenario from the theater of nature and natural disaster and climate change into the theater of war, the picture only darkens, the suffering only intensifies. The poor we will always have with us, yes—and always, it seems, the same poor, largely ignored until disaster strikes.

For Sobrino, what all this must elicit is a response, a revulsion against suffering, not in and of itself, but because so much of it is caused by human factors that render it avoidable. A "theology of suffering" would therefore involve a protest against suffering: a prophetic "no" that doubles as a summons to bring it to an end. This suffering on the cross of the poor—their dismissal by the rich—must cease, and the work of the Gospel must begin: to take the crucified peoples down from their crosses.[13] As an interruption and alleviation of suffering, this is an image of mercy toward the afflicted; but it is also an image of judgment on those who have wrought so much suffering, for the cross itself keeps alive the "dangerous memory" of the crucified.[14] This is one reason why Christians post a cross on their walls, or wear a cross around their necks—always to remember and never to forget the cost of suffering.[15] But Sobrino intends something even more by the use of this image: a remaking of our image of the cross by seeing on it the people who suffer at the hands of injustice. It is not suffering itself that is at issue: it is the suffering that issues from injustice. And the image of taking the crucified peoples down from their crosses is intended to address this fundamental fact. It is to join in God's emphatic *no!* to such suffering wrought by injustice, and God's judgment against it.

The themes sketched here are found in many places in Sobrino's work. Perhaps the most succinct summary is in his essay "The Crucified Peoples: Yahweh's Suffering Servant Today," an essay written in memory of his martyred Jesuit companion Ignacio Ellacuría and in anticipation of 1992, the quincentenary of the arrival of the Spanish in the Americas.[16] In this essay Sobrino describes the "horrifying fact" of the inhuman poverty and misery in which so many people live, the marginalization of the poorest of the poor (especially indigenous peoples), and the crucifixion by impoverishment and disease that leads to actual death for so many. Like Ellacuría, Sobrino sees the crucified peoples as the contemporary embodiment of the Suffering Servant, and thus as bearers of salvation.[17]

Yet it is "we," the noncrucified (and, in some cases, the crucifiers) who can decide whether to bring the crucified people down from the cross. Failure to do so brings judgment upon us, because among the noncrucified are those who are responsible for so much injustice, and those who witness such injustice without protest—virtually all of the rest of us. Solidarity, then, is the requirement of an "anthropodicy by which human beings can be justified"—by which those of us who are called into solidarity can be justified.[18] If, according to Johannes Metz, the question for theology after the genocide of the Jews by the Nazis in World War II was how to justify God, a question strictly speaking of theodicy, the question for the tragedy of Latin America and other tragic lands and peoples is how to justify the human beings who have been the cause of so much tragedy, or who have been the "shuffling bystanders" who look away. The only way the perpetrators or bystanders can be vindicated (from a human standpoint) is if they are converted to a new vision for humanity and for themselves, and begin to take the crucified down from their crosses, thus working for the integral liberation of the suffering poor, rather than the continuing oppression that has resulted in death.

Sobrino is essentially calling for a conversion of the way we understand our Christian vocation and the vocation of the church. This degree of conversion would seem to be rare, but not impossible. He cites the shift of Archbishop Oscar Romero of San Salvador, from a position of quiet upholder of the status quo, to a prophetic leader of the crucified people and a stalwart defender of their dignity and rights. A humble leader who gave voice to the poor in El Salvador, he was shot dead while celebrating Mass in a hospital chapel. But the solidarity of taking the crucified down from their crosses is what Romero implicitly invoked at El Paisnal (quoted at the head of this chapter) when he told them, "You are the image of all people, who like yourselves, have been pierced and abused. But if you suffer this pain with faith, then you will give your suffering a redemptive meaning." He had arrived at this insight through his own process of gradual conversion to stand with his people, in solidarity with them, the suffering body of Christ in his time.

But here enters a crucial twist. For those who show the way

to conversion and toward solidarity are the crucified peoples themselves. Without wishing to romanticize the poor, Sobrino nevertheless suggests that the crucified peoples offer the rest of us a sense of hope, a demonstrated solidarity, and a testament to faith as church that the powerful and privileged have much to learn from.[19] This does not mean that the suffering poor do not sin or that they are not themselves in need of personal conversion. But Sobrino wants to emphasize that they are, nevertheless, instruments of salvation, precisely because their impoverishment and weakness challenges all of us to ask how we are living our lives, and what it would mean to bring an end to the suffering that results from such tragic human states. And so he concludes: "It is paradoxical, but it is true. The crucified peoples offer light and salvation."[20] But there is a deeper reason for stating this: for "a crucified people resembles Jesus by the mere fact of what it is and is loved preferentially by God because of what it is. . . . The reality of the act of faith in Christ comes about in this reproducing of his features, in this becoming daughters and sons in the Son."[21]

The crucified peoples, then, give us an insight into Jesus, the innocent one, made to "be sin" (2 Cor 5:21) by the powers that prosecuted him. The sense of abandonment expressed by Jesus on the cross raises fundamental challenges to our most cherished ideas about God as loving and present to us in our own sufferings.[22] This "profound isolation" of Jesus in turn, marked a "theological discontinuity" between Jesus's entire life of absolute closeness to God, and now, this nightmare of infinite distance and radical dislocation: in his hour of greatest need, Jesus encounters only the silence of God. This, in turn, reveals to us something about suffering itself, which "remains the supreme enigma for human reason."[23] Here Sobrino confronts the harsh reality of suffering, and its offensiveness: the impossibility of our finding final meaning in it—a fact made more forceful when we are considering the suffering of innocent people or people whose suffering is caused by nothing they have called upon themselves.

What, then, do we make of the silence of God? For throughout all this human drama, all this tragedy, God does seem remote. To take up the theodicy question, how do we fit God into all of this? Sobrino arrives at a position that is neither apologetic (God is in no way involved) nor accommodationist (God somehow bore the sufferings of the cross). Rather, squarely facing the silence of God, Sobrino suggests that "God suffered on Jesus's cross and on those of this world's victims by being their non-active and silent witness."[24] For if God allowed God's very Self to become incarnate in the sinfulness of human reality and history, then God also submitted to the limitations of that condition. The silence of God is in some sense an indication of the "weakness" of God, for God has entered into solidarity with the suffering victims of history, those who have no voice, who are themselves reduced to a silence in their suffering. But because this is a silence that issues from the serene freedom of God's compassion, God's desire to be with the suffering, it does not signal a resignation to suffering, but rather a profound divine sharing in the bearing of injustice. This divine sharing, and not any extrinsic program, theological or political, is the deepest foundation of a way of being Christian in the world, of being an agent of liberating those who need it. "In Latin America it is a tangible fact that God's suffering has also been an idea that has encouraged liberation rather than resignation."[25] The suffering silence of God, mirrored in the silence of Jesus himself as he went to the cross, is a powerful unmasking of the "illegitimate interests" that caused such suffering in the first place. This solidarity of the "lesser God," the God of solidarity with the powerless, is in fact a kind of protest against the crucifixions of the world even as God silently bears the pain of such crucifixions.[26]

This is a God who is freely unmoored—who is dislodged from the heights of the heavens, and who descends into, and assumes the state of, the suffering and powerless—those without anything to cling to for security or fixity. The unmoored God is now to be understood not as a distant God, but as the silent God who draws near in compassion, tenderness, and a desire to save.

And here we enter into a new phase of Sobrino's Christology. From the cross of Jesus and God's solidarity with Jesus in the divine silence, we must ask what the Resurrection might mean in this context. Sobrino treats this in the second volume of his Christology, whose original Spanish title could be literally translated as "Faith in Jesus Christ: An Essay from the Victims." (The title of the official English translation is *Christ the Liberator: A View from the Victims.*)[27] Sobrino's prism is the "victims" of history, a term he uses here in preference to "the poor," which he had used earlier. Why? He wishes to emphasize that the "poor" are the "impoverished"—a term used to emphasize that poverty is the result of conditions forced upon people. To be poor is not a natural state. As such, the impoverished are victims—they are made to be poor. These victims of history include especially those who are economically poor, because this fundamental type of poverty is caused by an inequality that issues from the indifference of the rich, and by institutionalized hypocrisy at many levels. Sobrino therefore claims that poverty "is the most lasting form of violence and the violence that is committed with the greatest impunity."[28] It is from the viewpoint and experience of the victims, that Sobrino will undertake an interpretation of the Resurrection and of its relation to the sufferings of the cross and to the ongoing saving work of Christ in the world.

It is first important to note that the Resurrection of Jesus is an eschatological accomplishment of God's love—that is, it signals a final reality that is not yet fully realized but that has nevertheless been established. This means that suffering and death remain with us even as the power of God's love is working itself out within human history. The victims of history are still suffering, and so they present a reality that must figure into our understanding of the Resurrection. Still, the Resurrection is also the source of hope for people of Christian faith, that our future resides in God, and that it is life, not death, that God desires for us. If the Resurrection is the final cause of our hope, because it symbolizes and realizes God's desire for us, then how do we bring the horizon of the suffering victims of the world into relation with the horizon of hope that the resurrection of the dead signals? Isn't there something fanciful about this whole idea?

Sobrino's survey of Scripture in this work offers the beginning of an answer to this question. In ancient Israel, resurrection stood in opposition to "the tragedy of ending in *sheol*," which was tantamount to "ceasing to be in communion with [the Lord]."[29] For Israel, therefore, the promise of resurrection was the promise that the silence of God would not be eternal, that God would once again speak to Israel and enter into communion with God's beloved people, and within history. They would be established as a people, secure in their own land. But resurrection also spoke of a hope of communion with God beyond death. The fidelity of God to Israel resulted in Israel's faith in God's eternal fidelity—the "lordship of Yahweh" beyond history in a way that overcame the finality of death itself. And this triumph over death established God's "eschatological triumph over injustice," not only beyond death, but also in the present moment. Here Sobrino reminds us that resurrection in the Hebraic imagination is not the event that happens to an individual, but to of a whole people.[30] The resurrection of the dead, therefore, is the salvation of a whole people, a salvation that begins within history and comes to fulfillment in God's future.

And this has a definite effect on the fate of the victims of history, those who suffer but live in hope. This hope of the victims, which is more than hope for a mere survival, is nevertheless a "hope against hope" because of the darkness of suffering that enshrouds them. And, it must be added, not every Christian is a victim of history in precisely the way the impoverished of the world are victims. Yet the hope of the victims cannot somehow be a hope that is other than the hope of all Christians for eternal life. The question arises, then, as to how hope for *my* resurrection has anything to do with the hope of the victims for resurrection from what is already a living death, which is a living scandal. How can the words of Paul ring true: "I am now rejoicing in my sufferings for your sake, and in my flesh I am completing what is lacking in Christ's afflictions for the sake of his body, that is, the church" (Col 1:24)?

Sobrino's answer is challenging: "The Christian courage to hope in one's own resurrection depends on the courage to hope for the overcoming of the historical scandal of injustice. . . . The question is whether God can do justice to the victims produced by human beings."[31] The power of the Resurrection as an eschatological event is, therefore, going to be tied to the way the Resurrection is worked out in history, through the agency of the living body of Christ, the whole church. It will depend in part on the degree to which those who are not victims can participate in God's loving response to the victims of history, how they can undertake a "praxis" of resurrection—a way of enacting the hope of the Resurrection in human life. This means that we have, in Ignacio Ellacuría's words, to "take the situation on ourselves," in this case the situation of the victims; but it is also true that "the situation takes us on itself" and that it offers us not only sin and the obligation to eradicate it but also grace and the courage to hope. This is possible, Sobrino tells us, because "the victims offer us their hope."[32] And we have already seen why he finds "light and salvation" in the crucified people.

Christians live within the power of the Resurrection through what Sobrino calls "the praxis of raising the crucified." The pattern was set by the apostles, who are described in the Gospels and in the Acts of the Apostles as witnesses to the Resurrection—witnesses entrusted with a mission to further work out its reality and impact, by healing the sick, giving comfort to the afflicted, even raising the dead (Acts 9:39–41; 20:7–12). The Resurrection event is not limited to the accounts of the appearances of Jesus and the empty tomb; it is further realized in the ministries of the witnesses who are commissioned by the gift of the Spirit to carry out the work of the risen Christ. Sobrino explains that the "apostolate" of the disciples, what we might call the ministry each disciple discovers for herself or himself, is the key to understanding the Resurrection; without an apostolate, a way of enacting the hope of the Resurrection in life, the very nature of the Resurrection cannot be understood.[33] Praxis is the expression of the hope that motivates the witnesses to history who are also witnesses to the Resurrection of Jesus.

How does the Christian make this Resurrection praxis a reality? We can do so, first, by proclaiming the Resurrection through "putting oneself at the service of the resurrection" by working "in the service of eschatological ideals: justice, peace, solidarity, the life of the weak, community, dignity, celebration, and so on."[34] These are "partial resurrections" that help realize in human history the eschatological reality of the Resurrection. Further, this means undertaking courses of action that will bring about social, political, and economic transformation of the structures that have caused so much suffering and have created victims. In this kind of work, the Resurrection is the disclosure of the Reign of God, itself an eschatological vision of God's triumph, and the reversal of the programs of death and disintegration that led to the crucifixion in the first place. "And this is also what Ellacuría meant when he . . . used the expression 'taking the crucified people down from the cross' as a formulation of Christian mission."[35] Taking the crucified down from the cross is, therefore, an expression of Resurrection praxis. It is the most hope-filled activity, positively oriented toward life, that a Christian can imagine. It is the most radical expression of hope in the saving power of God made manifest on the suffering of the cross and vindicated in the symbol of the bodily resurrection of Jesus, his having been raised from the dead.

This theology will always thus pose a challenge to those who would wish to keep at arm's length the entire problem of the suffering caused by injustice, and what we are to do about it. It may well be that only this vision of faith, or one like it, can bring an end to the shuffling of the bystanders, the evasions of us priests and Levites (Lk 10:31–32) who pass the suffering on the road. Christian faith, and the demands of history, will not allow us to escape these questions or our responsibilities as people with breath and life. In Sobrino's terms, we are each now called upon at this moment in history to learn what it means to help take the crucified down from their crosses.

5

The Dislocation of Discipleship

> I never thought I would go to another country. That was never in my mind. . . . I did not think I needed to leave my home just for telling the truth. . . . My life changed in one moment to another moment, immediately. That is fast. Big change.
>
> —Lucia Cerna
>
> La Verdad: A Witness to the Salvadoran Martyrs

On November 16, 1989, Lucia Cerna was eye witness to one of the most heinous acts of the civil war in El Salvador—the slaying of six Jesuits, their housekeeper, and the housekeeper's daughter, in San Salvador, on the campus of the University of Central America. On the night of an opposition offensive against San Salvador, Lucia, also a housekeeper for the Jesuit community, sought safe haven with her husband, Jorge, and their daughter, Geraldina, in the Jesuit residence. They heard the gun shots and cries during the ruthless murder and caught glimpses of the soldiers from the darkness of their hiding place. The next day, well aware that the Salvadoran military would attempt to eliminate any witnesses, Lucia stepped forward to tell her story. As a woman of faith and a human being of integrity she chose the path that she believed was given to her to follow, agonizing though it was. In doing so, her life was changed forever. The Cerna family was rushed out of El Salvador and eventually to the United States, where her saga continued. She was forced through a wormhole into a new and very different world—all for following the path of discipleship.

It led to her physical relocation and permanent dislocation from what had been her family's home for many generations.

* * *

What I have been describing up to now is the situation of faith in a world of multiple dislocations: the dislocation of God from that world and God's self-dislocation into the chaos of it all, into a world of suffering, in the person of Jesus, God incarnate and crucified. And, as also noted, this situation of faith today makes believing difficult for many. How can we rediscover the God who has become so hard to locate? I have discussed one crucial part of the path: joining in solidarity with the crucified peoples of history, just as the God of Jesus Christ suffered dislocation in order to join in solidarity with the suffering of the world. In this chapter I consider another dimension of believing: the discovery of God through the dislocation of being a disciple of Jesus. It is within the actual experience of allowing ourselves to be changed, to lose our familiar bearings, that we can discover what it means to believe. This is where solidarity leads us—to a lived discipleship with no firm, underlying guarantees of stability, once the mantle has been accepted. In this form of discipleship, the unmoored God finds us in the newness of surrender to the suffering of others. And, through the examples that follow in this chapter, I suggest that this form of discipleship is what lies at the heart of what we mean by the church, that gathering of disciples who strive to follow the patterns of Jesus.

But first a brief word about discipleship itself.

The German biblical scholar Gerhard Lohfink explores the notion of living as a disciple as reflected in the various writings of the New Testament.[1] In surveying the gospels in particular, he makes two very important points. First, "discipleship" never appears as a noun in the gospels. "There is no such thing in the gospels as abstract discipleship. It is not an idea or a purely inward disposition; it exists only as a concrete, visible, tangible event."[2] It is an activity, literally, a "walking behind" the teacher. Following Jesus involves learning how to enact his message by living it. To believe in Jesus is not simply to claim adherence to a doctrine or a set of beliefs, nor even to remembering all his teachings; it is to enter into his entourage by *living* his teaching of the Reign of God and thereby participating in his mission. It is not a matter of following a particular theological school or even becoming a devotee of a particular spirituality, but rather of conforming oneself, as much as possible, to the person of the teacher, Jesus.

Second, this form of participation in Jesus's mission takes many paths, and each of them works in harmony with the others to achieve the mission of the Gospel. This is not a "lone ranger" ethos; to be a disciple is to be part of an ecclesial reality, a gathering of disciples. The entire church allows itself to suffer dislocation in service of those who themselves have been most severely dislocated by the harsh blows of historical events. Each disciple, in communion with all other disciples, is called by baptism to join in solidarity in mission as the church in the world, albeit in different ways.[3] That said, each person has a unique history, with an individual ability or inability to see, an individual freedom or lack of freedom. This individual history helps form the calling of each person. Only those who see the distortions of history find themselves called to enter into solidarity with those who suffer from these distortions. But no one is called to something that is completely outside his or her sphere of possibilities. No one can be called to respond to every form of suffering, but callings to various forms of discipleship can work together to form the whole of the people of God, the church.

How can we begin to imagine discipleship for ourselves? I approach this question through consideration of three dimensions of discipleship, offered by three disciples: the Protestant theologian Dietrich Bonhoeffer's following of Jesus even to martyrdom, Jesuit theologian Karl Rahner's living of faith in what he calls the "diaspora," and Anglican theologian Kathryn Tanner's understanding of Christian discipleship as distributing the gifts of God. Each develops a different dimension of discipleship, appropriate to the situation of many people today who struggle with believing and for whom dislocation, human or divine, of any sort might seem to be a frightening prospect for faith.

* * *

Dietrich Bonhoeffer, a German theologian and Lutheran pastor, was one of the great Christian witnesses of our time. Born into a prosperous middle-class German family, he was something of a theological prodigy and made rapid progress in academic theology. He was also a gifted pastor and preacher. His youthful pursuit of his calling as a pastor and scholar occurred just as Hitler's Third Reich was emerging as a dark reality. Bonhoeffer and a group of like-minded Christians grew increasingly alarmed over the directions Hitler was taking, and the complicity of the German Lutheran Church (which was the established state church) in the advancement of Nazi propaganda within and beyond the life of the church itself. Bonhoeffer considered that what was happening within the church was nothing short of idolatry, an abdication of the God of Jesus Christ and what the Gospel requires of disciples of Jesus. He and a group of others established a clandestine seminary in Finkenwalde, located in the remote German countryside, for what they called the Confessing Church—the church that would persist in affirming (confessing) faith in Jesus Christ and following the consequences of that faith in faithful and risk-laden discipleship. The charter for the church was composed by the great Protestant theologian Karl Barth and placed the church squarely in opposition to the regime of the Third Reich.[4]

Finkenwalde was to become a kind of model for Christian discipleship, where some of the fundamentals of a community among disciples were practiced. Bonhoeffer summarized these fundamentals in his little book, *Life Together*.[5] One salient dimension of ecclesial life that he presents here is its horizontality: hierarchical order is replaced by a community of disciples who mutually support and uphold one another. This carries over even into the sacrament of Confessing, where confession of sin is made from one disciple to another, neither of whom need be ordained. This communion of hearts and minds, rooted in opposition to the hierarchical ordering of Christianity that had resulted in the abdication of the Gospel to an alien ideology, was to strengthen the disciples in the Confessing Church for facing the fiercest forms of evil.

The Confessing Church was to prove true to its convictions, and some of its members decided, after deep consultation and prayer, to participate in a plot to overthrow Hitler through assassination. When the plot failed, Bonhoeffer, who had knowledge of it but was actually only indirectly related to it, was among those arrested. Just weeks before the end of the war and the liberation of Germany, he was hanged. He is revered today as a martyr by Protestants and Catholics alike, and he is one of those rare theologians whose personal experiences of life permeate almost every word of his writings.

While he was waiting in prison to face his fate, Bonhoeffer wrote a number of letters to his family, his friends, and to his fiancée, Renate. They have been published in the volume titled *The Letters and Papers from Prison.*[6] In a letter to his friend Eberhard Bethge, Bonhoeffer wrote the following:

> What is bothering me incessantly is the question what Christianity really is, or indeed who Christ really is, for us today. The time when people could be told everything by means of words, whether theological or pious, is over, and so is the time of inwardness and conscience—and that means the time of religion in general. We are moving towards a completely religionless time; people as they are now simply cannot be religious any more.[7]

By the curious phrase, "inwardness and conscience," Bonhoeffer was referring to a purely inward-looking religious pietism and the abdication of conscience he had witnessed in the German Protestant church. The era of a purely private, bourgeois religiosity was finished. Bonhoeffer explores this idea of a religionless time in a series of questions:

> What do a church, a community, a sermon, a liturgy, a Christian life mean in a religionless world? How do we speak of God—without religion, i.e., without the temporally conditioned presuppositions of metaphysics, inwardness, and

> so on? How do we speak (or perhaps we cannot now even "speak" as we used to) in a "secular" way about "God"? In what way are we "religionless-secular" Christians, in what way are we the *ek-klesia*, those who are called forth, not regarding ourselves from a religious point of view as specially favoured, but rather as belonging wholly to the world? In that case, Christ is no longer an object of religion, but something quite different, really the Lord of the world.[8]

Bonhoeffer was writing for what he called "a world come of age" in which "Man has learnt to deal with himself in all questions of importance without recourse to the 'working hypothesis' called 'God.'" And this extends even to religious questions, where "it is becoming evident that everything gets along without 'God'—and, in fact, just as well as before. As in the scientific field, so in human affairs generally, 'God' is being pushed more and more out of life, losing more and more ground."[9] By this, he meant that the God of theism that had been advanced by established Christianity no longer correlated with human experience. Europe was in upheaval, and God, too, was no longer in the old fixed places.

The result, Bonhoeffer saw, was the replacement of the true God with ideological idols, such as those of National Socialism. In such a situation, the forms of faith, what we call "religion," no longer function to serve faith in the God of Jesus Christ; they now exist to bolster ideologies. And so, faithful Lutheran that he was and that he remained to his death, Bonhoeffer also sensed that something new had to come about, an age of "religionless Christianity." He did not mean by this phrase that it was now fine to be "spiritual but not religious," a coinage of recent vintage and of very different meaning. Nor did he believe that it was possible to be a person of Christian faith without a church. What he did mean is that Christian faith needed to rediscover its radical nature by critiquing the ways that false religion had led to such immoral compromises and idolatries. And this meant that Christians, individually and as communities, needed to rediscover what discipleship of Jesus demands, which is, as he put it, costly.[10]

Although the churches may fail in their moral obligation to

examine their own idolatries masked as religion, nonetheless Christians cannot abdicate their responsibility to be faithful to Jesus Christ. At the root of the church is discipleship, a discipleship that becomes explicit within an ethical framework of the Gospel. Christian believing, therefore, is a critical undertaking of discipleship, and can involve rejection of forms of religion, including some teachings, that serve not the true God, not the "Lord of the world," but the idols of religious, social, or political ideologies. For Bonhoeffer, the God we must recover is the God of Jesus, who was the God of the covenant with Moses. This is a God who is near to God's people, empathic and compassionate in regard to their sufferings, and desiring what is good and true that will lead to their flourishing, planted in a Promised Land: the Kingdom of God in the preaching of Jesus. And so, in the crucible of his discipleship, which entailed suffering unto death, Bonhoeffer points the way to a rediscovery of God in a world come of age, in a Christianity emancipated from the bourgeois limitations of religion and its institutions: a believing realized in radical discipleship of Christ, the Lord of the world, which is something larger than but also encompassing the institutions of the church. Bonhoeffer was willing to undergo the most radical form of dislocation in his single-minded pursuit of that kind of discipleship: the ultimate dislocation of martyrdom.

* * *

Some of this sense of a "world come of age" is evident in the work of Karl Rahner. Born just two years before Bonhoeffer, he was also a German who lived through the harrowing events of Europe during World War II. His student and a friend was fellow Jesuit Alfred Delp, who, like Bonhoeffer, was executed for his role in opposing the Third Reich—a death that deeply affected Rahner.[11] Rahner himself knew what it meant to find himself dislocated, as he and other Jesuits were expelled from their theological college in Innsbruck, Austria. Rahner was assigned to a residence in Vienna, where his work took a deeply pastoral turn, addressing the sudden needs faced by the Austrian church as a result of the war. One of his more moving pieces reflective of that period likens the state of the contemporary soul to those who find themselves buried in the rubble from the bombings:

> Many of us remember those long nights in an air-raid shelter during the war, when we stood in abysmal loneliness among a crowd of terror-stricken people, waiting for death. In the darkness, we felt the coldness of fear chilling our hearts, and it was in vain that we put on a show of courage and a stiff upper lip: our brave words were hollow, and fell as husks about our feet, leaving only silence. . . . Then the explosion came, and the shower of debris to bury us. Let this be taken as the symbol of modern life. We have indeed crawled out from the powdered shelters; we have resumed our daily lives with a great show of bravery and pretense of enjoyment; but the truth is that many of us are as though we had remained buried in the debris, because we have suffered no change of heart through having been brushed by the wing of death. However farfetched it may sound, it remains true that externals are but the shadow of what has taken place in the depths of our hearts. Our hearts are obstructed, buried under debris.[12]

After the war, much of Rahner's theology bore the stamp of his ongoing ruminations about the state of humankind in relation to God. I have already noted (in chapter 2) his thoughts about how we can speak of God at all and, more existentially, what should happen to human beings if we were to lose any sense of God, to forget even the word "God." Rahner's suggestion that we could ever forget the word "God" derives from his witnessing the dehumanization of Nazism, which was built on a radical displacement of God by a racist (anti-Semitic) and nationalist ideology. Rahner asks what it means to be a believer in a world such as this. The church, though necessary to the life of faith, is not in and of itself, qua institution, an object of faith. The forms of the institution can change, and need to change, and in many ways we could say that they are even now changing and, in some ways, imploding. The ruins of Cluny, in southern France, are a reminder that we have here on earth no lasting ecclesiastical city, and the ruination of many Christian churches today in places of persecution is proof positive that faith does not rest on these structures, venerable though they are in Christian memory.

Where Bonhoeffer spoke of a "world come of age," Rahner spoke of the "diaspora" situation of the modern Christian—that to be a Christian in the world today means that we no longer have a sense of homeland, of fixedness, not even always within the church itself, and certainly not within the worlds we inhabit. Like the Jews who were scattered after the destruction of the temple in 70 CE, Christians are scattered, existentially as well as sociologically and otherwise, from reassuring centers of religious orientation. Developments in the world, in society, in the church, and perhaps today we might add in nature itself, increasingly preclude a sense of a fixed home. The Christian is rootless, except in relation to his or her destiny in God, who is not the God of an abstract theism, but the God of mystery whom we so easily miss in easy talk about "God," as if we fully knew what we are referring to. For Rahner, God is the inexhaustibly knowable and silent one (Mystery), the source and finality of our existence, the one in whom all human beings "move and breathe and have their being" (Acts 17:28)—so radically close (holy) that this God can be missed in the divine hiddenness.[13] And so Christians constitute communities of witness to the Gospel in environments where the Gospel otherwise is given no attention or credence. And the individual Christian is often enough a silent witness to the Gospel, just by virtue of carrying on life in the midst of a wholly secularized environment.

But this very fact is an indication that God transcends the boundaries of religion. The walls that once set the church apart from the world have crumbled to the degree that if we really understand what Christian faith entails, then we can even speak of people who are anonymously Christian although they do not profess the faith as such, much less belong to the church through baptism. But they, in their own ways, affirm the nearness of God in their lives. For what drives the baptized Christian and the anonymous Christian is the dynamic between love of God and love of neighbor which takes us straight into the mystery of Christ and derives from it.[14]

When Rahner was writing, the Second Vatican Council had

concluded, but the pontificate of John Paul II would signal a spirit far different from that of John XXIII and of Paul VI, the popes of that council. In Rahner's eyes, the church was weathering a "wintry season." He was referring to the various signs of diminishment of vitality in the life of the church, at least in Europe at the time. The church was missing the boat, he felt, and not heeding the "signs of the times" and losing many of God's people as a result.[15] The church had lost sight of the radicality of faith, of the fact that faith in the God of Jesus Christ makes sense only in the context of the disruptions of life and of history, and that these disruptions—the final one being death itself—open us to the Mystery that we call God. The ecclesiastical winter Rahner described was tied to an institutional theological will to transcend or deny what is happening to people in history, a denial made in the name of a God who is perfect and demands that we be perfect, too, even if perfection is an impossibility. It is this kind of God who could no longer register for many, who felt far away. The result was often alienation and, worse, loss of any sense of God.

For Rahner, the true God, who has become elusive to so many, can be rediscovered through a life characterized by the radical risk of love that was originally given us in the self-emptying of God, as love, in Jesus, as so beautifully described by Johannes Metz. Jesus is the exemplar of a love and responsibility, the full acceptance of one's life before God. That fundamental self-acceptance, accepting that we are accepted,[16] is the condition upon which a Christian faith is lived out. All of this, he tells us, occurs not in some special religious sphere, but in the everyday of our lives, however unremarkable the details. Rahner writes:

> A Christian has the right and the obligation to give himself in trust and without reservations to the pluralism of his existence. He [or she] experiences both love and death, both success and disappointment. And through and in everything [one] can find in trust the very God who willed this incalculable pluralism in God's world.[17]

Believing thus becomes a way of living after the pattern of Jesus in this very world that God entered, in and through him.

* * *

Theologian Kathryn Tanner takes us straight into our current situation. If modernity, which unraveled during the twentieth century, was made of order, logistics, rationality, and clear and distinct goals, "postmodernity" is characterized by unpredictability and chaos (as represented by the counterintuitions of quantum mechanics), the dissolution of institutional boundaries, and a doubt about the finality of religious systems and even scientific doctrines. For example, today there are debates within evolutionary biology about whether evolution is directed toward any form of finality, or whether evolutionary processes are, in the bigger picture, unpredictable and sometimes regressive.[18] All of this entropy results in what could be called a very complex situation for Christian faith, in which no one context, much less one theology or understanding, can exhaust the meaning of it. No wonder, then, that for many people God seems so elusive, the church irrelevant, and believing a challenge. Yet in the midst of this situation Tanner forges a theological vision that is both solidly rooted in and faithful to the ancient traditions of faith while opening us up to new understandings of God and of the implications of believing in this God. She does not pretend to invent a vision of faith out of whole cloth. She is indebted in her project not only to Rahner but also to Aquinas, the Protestant Swiss theologian Karl Barth, and behind the text, to the contemporary postmodern French theologian Jean-Luc Marion, and those thinkers who are talking about the "return" of God.[19]

Tanner's vision of coming to know and believe in God borrows from these thinkers but rests on an understanding of who Jesus is. Christian faith holds that Jesus is the enfleshment of the divine, that in him the God-Mystery has been given fully, and that in him God has entered into a state of dislocation through a kenosis of self-giving. And what we see in this Jesus is something that we see in ourselves: a noncompetitive relation with the divine, and that our flourishing grows in direct proportion to God's largesse. The absolute transcendence of God implies that we are absolutely creatures, and exist by sheer dint of a gratuity that cannot be explained through ordinary human calculus. The divine outflow in creation, in us, in Christ, is nonpurposive. This differs from the standard Christian narrative, commonly attributed to Anselm, that the divine outflow occurs because of our human sinfulness; here it is a result only of the very nature of God, which is to reach toward the other in love—a part of the tradition that some Franciscan theologians, especially Duns Scotus, emphasized. But even this divine love is gratuitously given; God does not need to have loved in the way that God did. In this new narrative, God is the giver of God's very Self; the giver is the gift, which is itself a giving of the giver.[20] God is understood as the "giver of all good gifts, the foundation, luminous source, fecund treasury and store house. Like an 'overflowing radiance,' God 'sends forth upon all things . . . the rays of Its undivided Goodness'; 'the divine Goodness . . . maintains . . . and protects [all creation] and feasts them with its good things.'"[21] Giver/Giving/Gift is way of imagining this God, who is self-giving Mystery. Without this God, we would not exist. Yet this God lies outside chains of efficient causality, demonstration, or explanation.

But how is this Mystery disclosed? Again, we look to who Jesus is in relation to this God to find a theological structure for human life that will at once disclose the God-Mystery to us and give us indications about how to live. Here Tanner takes us into the depths of classical Christology, puzzling over the meaning of the ancient claims of Christian faith, drawing out the implications of the teaching that Jesus was fully human and fully divine. As shown in chapter 3, one principle she invokes, largely indebted to Rahner, is that in Jesus the self-gift of God is given in such a way that the recipient is not overpowered; there is, as just noted, a noncompetitive relation between the giver and the recipient. In fact, the recipient is brought to fulfillment, to a flourishing unto perfection, by dint of the gift, and grows in direct, not inverse, proportion to the gift. This is why Jesus can be said to be fully human, not less human, because of his relation with the divine. The more someone loves us, the more we are brought into the fullness of ourselves. This principle of Jesus's relation with the divine provides part of the theological structure of things—a way of seeing ourselves and, in so doing, somewhat like Christ, living out that relation between God's utterly gratuitous acts and being the recipient of them.

And how do we live it out? For Tanner discipleship is the exercise of the "ministry of divine benefits," distributing the goods of God to others in the solidarity of human community, acting as an "agent of God's own beneficence."[22] "By way of discipleship one helps distribute to the world all the gifts or blessings that follow from that primary gift of God's Self—life, beauty, goodness, bounty in the world."[23] And this distribution of the gifts is not tantamount to the good works of ordinary religion, which often involve some sort of redeeming moral purpose for the giver, a sense of inner satisfaction over being good, and an implicit acceptance of the status quo where one will always be in a position to give to those in need. No, here, giving "involves, not satisfaction with the status quo, but action against a reality that contradicts what is achieved in Christ's own glorified humanity; it involves resistance to a world of poverty and constriction, greed, and oppression."[24] It is a way of aligning ourselves with the self-giving nature of God, ultimately rooted in the trinity of relations that describes God as Mystery.

How does this approach, which is only sketched here, address the problem with which I began: the rediscovery of believing in a wary world where God has grown elusive? First, it addresses it by proposing an understanding of God that is the antithesis of the model of modern theism. This is a "weak" God whose strength lies not in power, but in *kenosis*, self-giving. Yet this is a sovereign God of mystery, one who gives of God's very Self out of sheer divine freedom, not out of some imputed need for us. Creation, and our very lives, are utterly gratuitous. In a very real sense—and this is hard for some people to take—God owes us nothing.[25] It is precisely because of this that a theologian such as Rahner can maintain that all is grace. Second, this is a God who speaks to an age of "religionlessness" and "diaspora," where people no longer feel anchored in the older models. Although Tanner hardly excludes the life of the church, particularly the Eucharist, that too depends radically on the God who transcends "godly" categories and whose mystery cannot be exhausted by the forms of religion against which people are understandably turning. Third, this is a God in whom we believe, not by assenting to propositions alone, but by living after the theological pattern disclosed by this God in Jesus, and particularly in his relations with the divine. He is the sheer self-expression of this Giving-Gift-Giver and, as Rahner would say, the full acceptance of it.

Where all of this leads is to a place very similar to what we find in the "Contemplation to Attain Divine Love," the final movement of the *Spiritual Exercises*. Here God is hardly the God of theism. We are back to the God of Moses, but now illuminated by what has been revealed in Jesus, who establishes the pattern of relationality with the Mystery. For "love consists of mutual sharing of goods"—a sharing "with the beloved what one possesses, or something of that which one has or is able to give."[26] This happens mutually between Jesus and the Mystery. And it is in this distribution of the gifts of love that one sees God in new ways, dwelling in creatures, sustaining all things in being, dwelling within me; and beyond this, sensing that I, and all of creation are radically dependent on God. For our existence is not necessary—it is gift. And, finally, there is the consideration of God as the Gift that is the Giver and the Giving: that all blessing and gifts are, as it were, descending from above like the glorious rays of the sun. This is a rediscovery of God that takes us out of the debates about the God of theism, beyond the sources of our alienation from religion, and plants it squarely in our experience of life, of ourselves as human beings, those who stumble from time to time upon burning bushes. It makes of believing a way of being, one of utter openness to the sheer mystery of the Gift, and following where it leads us, even if it changes everything and results in a dislocation so total as to constitute exile, as it did for Lucia Cerna.

And this takes us back to the heart of the church, discipleship. For the church is a community of people who have placed their faith in the dislocated God, because they themselves have known and know some form of dislocation, and wish to be in solidarity with all the dislocated, especially those most literally dislocated. And this desire, even if inchoate in the circumstances of life, has the potential to change one's life fundamentally. As Lucia Cerna put it, in describing her witness to the killings of the Jesuits: "Sometimes I even thank God we were there that night, for believe it or not, we were there."[27] She had entered more fully into solidarity with the dislocated than she could have ever imagined. *Why did you do this, she was once asked? "Because I have faith, because I believe. It is that simple."*[28]

Epilogue: Toward a Mystagogy of Believing

The fundamental problem I have been addressing in this book is what it means to believe in God in a situation of many dislocations, human and divine. But as a matter of fundamental theology, the classic framework for approaching the problem of belief is to distinguish between what is held in faith as the knowledge about God revealed in the person of Jesus Christ enshrined in Scripture and taught by the church (*fides quae creditur*), that is, the objective content of faith as transmitted in tradition, and the means by which this "content" of faith is appropriated in and through the personhood of the human being who enters into saving relationship with God through a personal faith in the God of Jesus Christ (*fides qua creditur*).[1] These are not two distinct tracks or ways of believing, but are distinguishable aspects of a single, unified act of faith realized in discipleship.[2] Yet that act cannot be adequately represented by the positive content of faith itself as it may be expressed in the form of beliefs—as creedal, dogmatic, or more generally doctrinal statements.[3] It is realized in the various ways and means, religious as well as everyday, by which that faith is appropriated and lived. Thus, believing is more than an intellectual assent to propositions (or "beliefs") through a reasoning process; it is also, and complementary with this, a deeper entry into the reality of faith's "content" in and through the transcendent depths of spiritual subjectivity, leading to personal transformation. And these two dimensions enjoy a fundamental unity with each other that constitute the single and courageous act of faith, of believing as such.

Yet this fundamental unity between *fides quae* and *fides qua* can be lost when we focus on either a propositional approach to belief[4] or on a subordination of belief to a vague and undefined sense of faith or spiritual sensibility that makes too sharp a distinction between faith and belief.[5] And both of these possibilities are reflected in contemporary theology. The task for theology, then, is to develop an approach to believing that avoids this kind of bifurcation and that both broadens and deepens what believing means so that the nonbelieving world—which includes some believers themselves in their inability to express their faith with intellectual conviction—can be addressed. In short, we need what Karl Rahner calls a theology that is at once both mystagogic and missionary: "The theology of the future will . . . be a missionary and mystagogic theology. . . . For in the future the Church will no longer be upheld by traditions that are unquestioningly accepted in secular society, or regarded as an integral element of that society."[6] Rahner proceeds to raise the kinds of questions that people in a secular world are asking of theology and, through theology, of faith itself:

> "What does this mean for me (and society)?" "How does this really affect me?" "How precisely can I myself really believe this?" Once such questions as these are raised . . . theology of itself will become something quite different from what it formerly was. It will of itself become more mystagogic, more missionary, and this is something which in practice is in accordance with the contemporary and future situation.[7]

So what is needed is a theology that unifies the content of faith (beliefs) with the experience of God in faith, in a deeper understanding of believing (the mystagogic task), thereby enabling Christian theology to function within and address people of the church and of the world who are steeped in a secular milieu (the missionary task). Believing involves not only intellectual assent to truth, but religious practice, and as I have tried to emphasize, entering into solidarity with the crucified peoples, and this in mode of discipleship of Jesus. Religious practice, then, entails living within the world according to the Gospel. In this way we might imagine how our ontological and existential dislocations might be met in the "home" who is God.

We begin with the ecclesial practices of the first century, when faith and belief were simultaneously expressed in the baptismal ritual, wherein an assent to faith was made with all one's being, including not only will but intellect. This assent was given symbolic expression in the baptismal dialogue, the simple and scripturally based formulae of faith known as the *regulae fidei*, and the early creeds that sprang from these formulae.[8] The formula was trinitarian: "Do you believe in God, the Father Almighty? Do you believe in God's only Son, Jesus Christ? Do you believe in the Holy Spirit?" But full assent to the beliefs of faith—a rational assent and not simply a matter of aspiration—was realized in an act of believing through participation in the liturgical mysteries, which was where faith received its mystagogical enactment. In this liturgical enactment, faith and believing were seen to constitute a unity with only a formal distinction, because the act of faith is realized in the mystagogy of believing, symbolically realized by the sacraments of baptism and Eucharist, which established and formed the Christian community as a body. And these involved conversion also of the heart, leading to changes in the way people lived their lives.

In something of an illustration of this principle, Michael C. McCarthy has discussed what he calls "modalities of belief" in early Christian debates, focusing on Augustine's arguments with the Pelagians, who had argued that human beings can work out their salvation without the benefit of God's grace.[9] In the theoretical grounding of his essay, McCarthy joins historians and cultural anthropologists in questioning the notion of belief as a carefully circumscribed set of doctrines with clear boundaries establishing insiders and outsiders, and argues instead for a notion of belief that is tied to communal practice and relationships.

> Like their Greco-Roman counterparts [the early] Christians too manifest modalities which inhabit a strange kind of space where they appear committed to the idea of a universal and coherent system of doctrines while resisting or even obfuscating its careful delineation. The anathemas of church councils imply that belief is a form of interior assent to some core doctrines that make up the universal

> "faith of the church," but the actual relationship between an individual's act of will and the surrounding culture is exceedingly complex.[10]

This is territory that McCarthy maintains has been little noticed, and it has indeed been a minority voice in theological treatments of doctrine and heresy, as it has been in patristic studies.[11] But it has not been lost to those immersed in the study of liturgical history and theology, nor to those engaged in ritual theory. Catherine Bell, a scholar in the history of religions whom McCarthy cites, is a major case in point, and her work in ritual theory and its relation to practice established a wider framework for consideration of the relationship between belief and the practice of faith.[12]

In several unpublished works, Bell examined the meaning of belief in early Christianity as well as in other religious systems.[13] First, it is clear that for the early Christians, belief was a matter of choice, usually following on conversion to the worldview of Christian faith, which included its beliefs, and which also involved a rejection of alternative beliefs: "I believe in this, not that; I am a Christian, not a Roman, not a Jew, ideally, not a master nor slave, male nor female. Being Christian was meant as the all-encompassing signifier."[14] It was this choice that led to a ritualized initiation into a community of shared vision and oral proclamation of a common faith in the form of the creeds.

Still, Bell questions the "choice and conversion of the individual" model on which this notion of belief rests. It leads to a Christian (and Western) particularism about what is meant by belief. Turning to Buddhism as a contrasting data field, Bell would take what she calls a "practice approach" to the matter, asking "about believing not belief or beliefs; we would ask how believing is constructed, with what imagery that distinguishes it in Dogon or Buddhist culture from other forms of thinking, philosophizing, etc."[15] This approach, she says, is more complicated than simply specifying particular beliefs (or doctrines), for it suggests a number of forms that believing might take, "a spectrum of distinguished forms and positions."[16] It expands believing from the private realm of an assent of intellect and will to a focus on religious practice—"the implicit expectations, the assumptions at stake, the crown jewels in the pocket of a particular view of reality " Practically, this would involve a methodology that would take into account the historical forms of religious commitment, including the texts, rituals, and ethical precepts that inform such a commitment. Theologically speaking, this would involve an examination of how faith is lived and what its ethical implications are. What this leads to, she says, is "that choice, commitment, rejection is not at all what Christian believing is about; that is what it wants one to think it is doing, not what it is really doing. Probably believing is more likely to be a way in which contradictions are maintained, not truths affirmed."[17] The issue, then, is not which "beliefs" comport with faith and how, but how faith is realized in patterns of believing, understood in a richly textured sense that includes "truths" of faith handed down through tradition and teaching, but not exhausted by that category.[18] Here we find some congruence with the thinking of Talal Asad, who, as we have seen, sees the "religious" or "sacred" as a fluid and shifting category where the essence of religious commitment is not found in beliefs as such, but in the mythological worlds within which people live their lives, both religious and secular.[19]

What I wish to suggest here is that a "mystagogy" of believing—believing that would give form and expression to faith—would be constituted by spiritual, doctrinal or theological, and institutional practices, all of which together constitute a coherent religious world that would not reduce God to a manageable idol. But these also constitute an actual community that is, both on the level of individuals and as a body, receptive to the "gift" of faith, that is, to the cultivation of the theological virtue of faith. Faith in a Christian sense does not point to a vague or undifferentiated God, but rather to a God who has self-communicated as Spirit and as Word-made-flesh. This is a God who has entered into the dislocation of the human condition through a divine self-dislocation. This is a God who is therefore, eminently personal, and who, in the form of a human being, embodies not only a message about God, but God's very Self to the human race. Faith is not in the message per se, nor first and foremost in its doctrinal or even liturgical expressions, much less in institutions that have arisen from the message; it is rather assent of the entire human person to the trinity of divine Persons—intellect, will, transcendent spirit, embodied being—who offers himself as "the way" to the mystery of God (see Jn 14:6). Christian faith, then, concerns not only "God" as in the ineffable term of our transcendence, but "God" as the eminently personal, the one who, by virtue of being and existing, establishes the personal as the transcendent mystery of which we, human beings, are finite analogates.

As we have seen, discipleship takes many forms. Some literally followed Jesus on the road, adopting radical poverty with him, while others followed him by welcoming other followers into their homes and maintaining their regular lives. The point is that believing in Jesus is realized by participation in his mission, practicing the way of Jesus. This would involve interpretation, both personal and communal, as the early church developed, and we can see the ensuing development of doctrine as a sign of that process. But underlying this is the mystagogy of believing that begins in the baptism of Christians, giving them the ability to "see" Jesus. Following this baptismal vocation is the primary mode of Christian believing in God. Furthermore, discipleship—or participation in the mission of Jesus—involves an act of self-transcendence in giving oneself over to God by giving oneself over to the other. This act of self-transcendence does not abandon the personal, but finds it not only in the categories of religion, but also beyond those categories, in the yearnings and unanswered questions raised by those who claim no faith, as well as by those who do. We see this in the gospels themselves, as when Jesus meets the Samaritan woman (Jn 4:1–42) who comes to see who Jesus is, even while remaining a Samaritan; or even inside Israel, as in his fraternal conversation with the inquisitive Nicodemus (Jn 3:1–21), where believing in the truth is said to coincide with living (doing deeds) in the light of God. These approaches to the nonbeliever or seeker in the gospels model engagement with both nonbelievers and questioners in our own time, and model also the dynamism of believing understood as a mystagogy of practice. The Emmaus story (Lk 24:13–35) expresses this directly, when the two disciples invite into their company a stranger who does not know what has happened in Jerusalem. When their eyes are opened at the breaking of the bread, they change course and head back toward Jerusalem, on mission. Discipleship, then, can be understood as a mode of believing, a mystagogy of believing, that reaches beyond oneself toward the dislocated strangers, draws them into dialogue, moves along the road with them, and explores the depths of what we hold in belief. But, more than discoursing about beliefs, it is a moving along the road of life, breaking bread with the other, and transcending our limited selves with burning hearts, meeting the other where *cor ad cor loquitur*, "heart speaks unto heart."

Here, then, we find grounds for believing again. For it is here, in the communion of hearts in love, that God, who has otherwise been so distant, so unmoored—because we have been—now finds a home.

Bibliography

Alfaro, Juan. "Faith." In *Encyclopedia of Theology: The Concise* Sacramentum Mundi, edited by Karl Rahner, 500–510. New York: Seabury, 1975.

Anselm of Canterbury. *St. Anselm: Basic Writings*. Translated by S. N. Deane. LaSalle, IL: Open Court, 1968.

Anderson, Bernard W. *Understanding the Old Testament*. 2nd ed. Englewood Cliffs, NJ: Prentice-Hall, 1966.

Asad, Talal. *Formations of the Secular: Christianity, Islam, Modernity*. Stanford, CA: Stanford University Press, 2003.

Augustine of Hippo. *Confessions*. Translated by Henry Chadwick. Oxford: Oxford University Press, 1991.

Bell, Catherine. *Ritual Theory/Ritual Practice*. New York: Oxford University Press, 1992.

Bellah, Robert. *Habits of the Heart*. Berkeley: University of California Press, 1998.

Bethge, Eberhard. *Dietrich Bonhoeffer: Theologian, Christian, Man for His Times: A Biography*. Rev. ed. Edited by Victoria J. Barnett. Translated by Eric Mosbacher. Minneapolis: Fortress Press, 2000.

Bonhoeffer, Dietrich. *The Cost of Discipleship*. Translated by Reginald Fuller and Irmgard Booth. New York: Macmillan, 1949.

———. *Letters and Papers from Prison*. Greatly enlarged edition. Translated by Reginald Fuller, Frank Clark, et al. Edited by Eberhard Bethge. New York: Macmillan, 1971.

———. *Life Together*. Translated by John W. Doberstein. New York: Harper and Row, 1954.

Bracken, Joseph. "God's Will or God's Desires for Us: A Change in Worldview?" *Theological Studies* 71 (2010): 62–78.

Brekelmans, Antonius. "Professions de foi dans l'eglise primitive:

Origine et fonction." *Concilium* 51, no. 1 (1970): 30.

Brown, Peter. *Augustine of Hippo*. Berkeley: University of California Press, 1967.

Buber, Martin. *Between Man and Man*. Translated by Ronald Gregor Smith. New York: Macmillan, 1965.

Buckley, Michael J. *At the Origins of Modern Atheism*. New Haven, CT: Yale University Press, 1987.

———. *Denying and Disclosing God: The Ambiguous Progress of Modern Atheism*. New Haven, CT: Yale University Press, 2004.

———. "The Rise of Modern Atheism and the Religious Epoché." *Proceedings of the Catholic Theological Society of America*, edited by Paul Crowley, 47 (1992): 69–83.

Caputo, John, and Michael J. Scanlon, eds. *God, the Gift, and Postmodernism*. Bloomington: Indiana University Press, 1999.

Cerna, Lucia, and Mary Jo Ignoffo. *La Verdad: A Witness to the Salvadoran Martyrs*. Maryknoll, NY: Orbis Books, 2014.

Chelala, César A. "Central America's Health Plight." *Christian Science Monitor*, March 22, 1990. See http://www.csmonitor.com/1990/0322/echel.html.

Crowley, Paul. "Between Earth and Heaven: Ignatian Imagination and the Aesthetics of Liberation." In *Through a Glass Darkly: Essays in the Religious Imagination*, edited by John C. Hawley. New York: Fordham University Press, 1996.

———. "*Instrumentum Divinitatis* in Thomas Aquinas: Recovering the Divinity of Christ." *Theological Studies* 52 (1991): 451–75.

———. "Mystagogy and Mission: The Challenge of Nonbelief and the Task of Theology." *Theological Studies* 76 (2015): 7–28.

———. *Rahner beyond Rahner: A Great Theologian Encounters the Pacific Rim*. Lanham, MD: Rowan and Littlefield/Sheed and Ward, 2005,

———. "Theology in the Light of Human Suffering: A Note on 'Taking the Crucified Down from the Cross.'" In *Hope and Solidarity: Jon Sobrino's Challenge to Christian Theology*, edited by Stephen J. Pope. Maryknoll, NY: Orbis Books, 2008.

———. *Unwanted Wisdom: Suffering, the Cross, and Hope*. New York: Continuum, 2005.

Davies, Oliver, Paul D. Janz, and Clemens Sedmak. *Transformation Theology: Church in the World*. London: T&T Clark, 2007.

Delp, Alfred. *The Prison Meditations of Father Delp*. Introduction by Thomas Merton. New York: Herder and Herder, 1963. Reprinted as *Alfred Delp, SJ: Prison Writings*. Maryknoll, NY: Orbis Books, 2004.

Dumas, André. *Dietrich Bonhoeffer: Theologian of Reality*. Translated by Robert McAfee Brown. New York: Macmillan, 1968.

Dunn, Geoffrey D. "Heresy and Schism according to Cyprian of Carthage." *Journal of Theological Studies* 55 (2004): 551–74.

Endean, Philip. *Karl Rahner and Ignatian Spirituality*. Oxford: Oxford University Press, 2001.

Ernst, Harold E. "The Theological Notes and the Interpretation of Doctrine." *Theological Studies* 63 (2002): 813–25.

Fletcher, Jeanine Hill. "Rahner and Religious Diversity," in *The Cambridge Companion to Karl Rahner*, ed. Declan Marmion and Mary E. Hines. Cambridge: Cambridge University Press, 2005.

Francis, Pope. *Laudato Si'*. http://w2.vatican.va/content/francesco/en/encyclicals/documents/papa-francesco_20150524_enciclica-laudato-si.html.

———. "To Have Courage and Prophetic Audacity: Dialogue of Pope Francis with the Jesuits Gathered in the 36th General Congregation," October 24, 2016, http://www.laciviltacattolica.it/articoli_download/extra/DIALOGOPAPA_ENG.pdf.

Gadamer, Hans-Georg. *Truth and Method*. 2nd rev. ed. Translated by Joel Weinsheimer and Donald G. Marshall. New York: Crossroad, 1989.

Gaucher, Guy. *The Passion of Thérèse of Lisieux*. Translated by Anne Marie Brennan. New York: Crossroad, 1990.

Glover, Jonathan. *Humanity: A Moral History of the Twentieth Century*. New Haven, CT: Yale University Press, 2000.

Gregg, Robert, and Dennis Groh. *Early Arianism: A View of Salvation*. Philadelphia: Fortress Press, 1981.

Guardini, Romano. *Pascal for Our Time*. Translated by Brian Thompson. New York: Herder, 1960.

Habermas, Jürgen. *An Awareness of What Is Missing: Faith and*

Reason in a Post-Secular Age. Translated by Ciaran Cronin. Malden, MA: Polity Press, 2011.

Haight, Roger. *Dynamics of Theology*. 2nd ed. Maryknoll, NY: Orbis Books, 2001.

Heidegger, Martin. "Memorial Address." In *Discourse on Thinking*, translated by John M. Anderson and E. Hans Freund. New York: Harper Torchbooks, 1966.

Heyer, Kristin. *Kinship across Borders: A Christian Ethic of Immigration*. Washington, DC: Georgetown University Press, 2012.

Hick, John. *Evil and the God of Love*. Rev. ed. San Francisco: HarperSanFrancisco, 1977.

Ignatius of Loyola. *The Spiritual Exercises of St. Ignatius: A Literal Translation and a Contemporary Reading*. Edited by David Fleming. St. Louis: Institute of Jesuit Sources, 1978.

———. *The Spiritual Exercises of Saint Ignatius*. Translated by George E. Ganss. Chicago: Loyola University Press, 1992.

John Paul II, Pope. "Redemptor Hominis." Encyclical of April 3, 1979.

Johnson, Elizabeth A. *Quest for the Living God*. New York: Continuum, 2005.

Johnston, Mark. *Saving God: Religion after Idolatry*. Princeton, NJ: Princeton University Press, 2009.

Kearney, Richard. *Anatheism: Returning to God after God*. New York: Columbia University Press, 2010.

Keenan, James F. *The Works of Mercy: The Heart of Catholicism*. 2nd ed. Lanham, MD: Rowman and Littlefield, 2008.

Kolakowski, Leszek. *God Owes Us Nothing: A Brief Remark on Pascal's Religion and on the Spirit of Jansenism*. Chicago: University of Chicago Press, 1995.

Kuhn, Thomas S. *The Structure of Scientific Revolutions*. 2nd enl. ed. Chicago: University of Chicago Press, 1970.

Kushner, Tony. *Angels in America, Part Two: Perestroika*. Rev. ed. New York: Theater Communications Group, 1996,

Lafont, Ghislain. *Imagining the Catholic Church: Structured Communion in the Spirit*. Translated by John J. Burkhard. Collegeville, MN: Liturgical Press, 2000.

Lassalle-Klein, Robert. *Blood and Ink: Ignacio Ellacuría, Jon Sobrino, and the Jesuit Martyrs of the University of Central America.* Maryknoll, NY: Orbis Books, 2014.

Leo I, Pope. "First Christmas Sermon." In *Christ and His Mission: Christology and Soteriology*, edited by James M. Carmody and Thomas E. Clarke. Westminster, MD: Newman Press, 1966.

———. "Letter to Flavian of Constantinople." In *The Christian Faith in the Doctrinal Documents of the Catholic Church*, edited by Jacques Dupuis. New York: Alba House, 2001.

Lindbeck, George. *The Nature of Doctrine: Religion and Theology in a Post-Liberal Age.* Louisville, KY: Westminster John Knox Press, 1984.

Lohfink, Gerhard. *Jesus of Nazareth: What He Wanted, Who He Was.* Translated by Linda M. Maloney. Collegeville, MN: Liturgical Press, 2013.

Marion, Jean-Luc. *God without Being.* Translated by Thomas A. Carlson. Chicago: University of Chicago Press, 1991.

———. "Metaphysics and Phenomenology: A Relief for Theology." In *The Visible and the Revealed*, translated by Christina M. Gschwandtner. New York: Fordham University Press, 2008.

Marsden, George M., and Bradley J. Longfield. *The Secularization of the Academy.* New York: Oxford University Press, 1992.

McCabe, Herbert. *God and Evil in the Theology of St. Thomas Aquinas.* New York: Continuum, 2010.

McCarthy, Michael C. "Modalities of Belief in Ancient Christian Debate." *Journal of Early Christian Studies* 17, no. 4 (2000): 605–34.

Mendelson, Michael. "Saint Augustine." *Stanford Encyclopedia of Philosophy.* Winter 2012 online edition.

Mercadante, Linda A. *Belief without Borders: Inside the Minds of the Spiritual but Not Religious.* New York: Oxford University Press, 2014.

Metaxas, Eric. *Bonhoeffer: Pastor, Martyr, Prophet, Spy.* Nashville, TN: Thomas Nelson, 2010,

Metz, Johannes. *A Passion for God: The Mystical-Political Dimension of Christianity.* Translated by J. Matthew Ashley. New York: Paulist Press, 1998.

———. *Poverty of Spirit*. Translated by John Drury. Rev. ed. Translated by Carole Farris. New York: Paulist Press, 1968, 1998.
Miller, Richard W., ed. *Suffering and the Christian Life*. Maryknoll, NY: Orbis Books, 2013.
Milton, John. *The Complete Poetry and Essential Prose of John Milton*. Edited by William Kerrigan, John Rumrich, and Stephen M. Fallon. New York: Modern Library, 2007.
Moritz, Joshua M. "Evolutionary Biology and Theological Anthropology." In *The Routledge Companion to Theological Anthropology*, edited by Joshua R. Farris and Charles Taliaferro, 45–56. New York: Routledge, 2016.
Murray, John Courtney. *The Problem of God, Yesterday and Today*. New Haven, CT: Yale University Press, 1964.
Nietzsche, Friedrich. *The Gay Science*. Translated by Walter Kaufmann. New York: Vintage, 1974.
Pascal, Blaise. *Blaise Pascal: Pensées*. Translated by A. J. Krailsheimer. Harmondsworth, Eng.: Penguin Books, 2966.
Phan, Peter C. "Deus Migrator—God the Migrant: Migration of Theology and Theology of Migration." *Theological Studies* 77 (2016): 845–68.
Pritchard, James B. *The Ancient Near East: An Anthology of Texts and Pictures*. Princeton, NJ: Princeton University Press, 2011.
Rahner, Hugo. *Ignatius the Theologian*. Translated by Michael Barry. New York: Herder, 1968.
Rahner, Karl. *Do You Believe in God?* Translated by Richard Stachan. New York: Newman Press, 1969.
———. *The Eternal Year*. Translated by John Shea. Baltimore: Helicon Press, 1964.
———. "The Faith of the Christian Church and the Doctrine of the Church." In *Theological Investigations* 14, translated by David Bourke. New York: Seabury, 1976.
———. "Faith between Rationality and Emotion." In *Theological Investigations* 16, translated by David Morland. London: Darton, Longman and Todd, 1979.
———. "Following the Crucified." In *Theological Investigations* 18, translated by Edward Quinn. New York: Crossroad, 1983.

———. *Foundations of Christian Faith*. Translated by William Dych. New York: Crossroad, 1978.

———. *On Prayer.* Collegeville, MN: Liturgical Press, 1993.

———. "Possible Courses for the Theology of the Future." In *Theological Investigations* 13, translated by David Bourke. New York: Crossroad, 1983.

———. "Reflections on Methodology in Theology." In *Theological Investigations* 11, translated by David Bourke. New York: Crossroad, 1983.

———. "The Teaching Office of the Church in the Present-Day Crisis of Authority." In *Theological Investigations* 12, translated by David Bourke. New York: Crossroad, 1982.

———. "What Is a Dogmatic Statement?" In *Theological Investigations* 5, translated by Karl-H. Kruger. Baltimore: Helicon Press, 1966.

———. "Why Does God Allow Us to Suffer?" In *Theological Investigations* 19, translated by Edward Quinn. New York: Crossroad, 1983.

———. "A 'Wintry' Church and the Opportunities for Christianity." In *Faith in a Wintry Season: Conversations and Interviews with Karl Rahner in the Last Years of His Life*, edited by P. Imhof and H. Biallowons, and translated by H. Egan. New York: Crossroad, 1991.

Ratzinger, Joseph. *Introduction to Christianity*. Translated by J. R. Foster. New York: Seabury, 1979.

Ricoeur, Paul. *The Symbolism of Evil*. Translated by Emerson Buchanan. Boston: Beacon Press, 1967.

Rilke, Rainer Maria. *The Unknown Rilke: Expanded Edition.* Translated by Franz Wright. Oberlin, OH: Oberlin College Press, 1990.

Rivera, Joseph. "God and Metaphysics in Contemporary Theology: Reframing the Debate." *Theological Studies* 77 (2016): 803–22.

Romero, Oscar. "A Torch Raised on High." Sermon, June 19, 1977, Aquilares, El Salvador, http://www.romerotrust.org.uk/homilies-and-writings/homilies/torch-raised-high.

Schillebeeckx, Edward. *The Schillebeeckx Reader*. Edited and

translated by Robert Schreiter. New York: Crossroad, 1987.
Schlesinger, Eugene R. "The Church's Eucharistic Poverty in the Theologies of Jon Sobrino and Hans Urs von Balthasar." *Theological Studies* 77 (2016): 627–51.
Schweizer, Bernard. *Hating God: The Untold Story of Misotheism*. New York: Oxford University Press, 2011.
Sewall, Richard B. *The Life of Emily Dickinson*. 2 vols. New York: Farrar, Straus and Giroux, 1974.
Smith, Christian, et al. *Young Catholic America: Emerging Adults In, Out of, and Gone from the Church*. New York: Oxford University Press, 2014.
Sobrino, Jon. *Christ the Liberator: A View from the Victims*. Translated by Paul Burns. Maryknoll, NY: Orbis Books, 2001.
———. *Jesus in Latin America*. Translated by Robert R. Barr. Maryknoll, NY: Orbis Books, 1987.
———. *Jesus the Liberator: A Historical-Theological View*. Translated by Paul Burns and Francis McDonagh. Maryknoll, NY: Orbis Books, 1993.
———. *The Principle of Mercy: Taking the Crucified People from the Cross*. Maryknoll, NY: Orbis Books, 1994.
———. *Spirituality of Liberation*. Maryknoll, NY: Orbis Books, 1989.
———. *Where Is God? Earthquake, Terrorism, Barbarity, and Hope*. Translated by Margaret Wilde. Maryknoll, NY: Orbis Books, 2004.
Southern, R. W. *St. Anselm: A Portrait in a Landscape*. Cambridge: Cambridge University Press, 1990.
Spivak, Gayatri Chakravorty. "Translator's Preface." Jacques Derrida, *Of Grammatology*. Baltimore: Johns Hopkins University Press, 1974.
Tanner, Kathryn. *Jesus, Humanity, and the Trinity: A Brief Systematic Theology*. Minneapolis: Fortress Press, 2001.
Taylor, Charles. *Dilemmas and Connections: Selected Essays*. Cambridge, MA: Belknap Press of Harvard University Press, 2011.
———. *A Secular Age*. Cambridge, MA: Belknap Press of Harvard University Press, 2007.
———. "Western Secularity." In *Rethinking Secularism*, edited

by Craig Calhoun, Mark Juergensmeyer, and Jonathan VanAntwerpen. New York: Oxford University Press, 2011.

Teresa of Calcutta. *Come Be My Light: The Private Writings of the Saint of Calcutta*. Edited by Brian Kolodiejchuk. New York: Doubleday, 2007.

Thiel, John. *God, Evil, and Innocent Suffering: A Theological Reflection*. New York: Crossroad, 2002.

Thomas Aquinas. *Summa Theologiae*. Madrid: Biblioteca de Autores Cristianos, 1951.

Tilley, Terrence W. *The Evils of Theodicy*. Washington, DC: Georgetown University Press, 1991.

Tillich, Paul. *The Shaking of the Foundations*. New York: Charles Scribner's Sons, 1948.

Traina, Cristina L. H. *Feminist Ethics and the Natural Law: An End to Anathemas*. Washington, DC: Georgetown University Press, 1999.

Vattimo, Gianni. *Belief*. Translated by Luca D'Isanto and David Webb. Stanford, CA: Stanford University Press, 1999.

———. "History of Salvation, History of Interpretation." In *The Return of God: Theological Perspectives in Contemporary Philosophy*, edited by Neils Grøhnkaer. Odense, Denmark: Odense University Press, 1998.

von Rad, Gerhard. *Old Testament Theology*, vol. 1: *The Theology of Israel's Historical Traditions*. Translated by D. M. G. Stalker. New York: Harper and Row, 1962.

Wall, Joseph. *The Providence of God in the Letters of St. Ignatius*. San Jose, CA: Smith-McKay, 1958.

Weil, Simone. *Waiting for God*. Translated by Emma Craufurd. New York: Harper and Row, 1951.

Wiman, Christian. *My Bright Abyss: Meditation of a Modern Believer*. New York: Farrar, Straus and Giroux, 2013.

Notes

Introduction

[1]See, for example, Linda A. Mercadante, *Belief without Borders: Inside the Minds of the Spiritual but Not Religious* (New York: Oxford University Press, 2014), and Christian Smith et al., *Young Catholic America: Emerging Adults In, Out of, and Gone from the Church* (New York: Oxford University Press, 2014).

[2]The United Nations High Commission on Refugees (UNHCR) estimates that there are currently "almost 60 million people forcibly displaced globally." The UNHCR distinguishes between refugees, "persons fleeing armed conflict or persecution," and migrants, who chose to move "mainly to improve their lives." See http://www.unhcr.org. The Internal Displacement Monitoring Centre in Geneva lists 38 million people displaced by conflict as of January 2015, and 19.3 million displaced by disasters in 1024, 86.5 percent of them in Asia. See http://www.internal-displacement.org. For an excellent analysis of the problem from the perspective of Catholic social teaching and theological ethics, particularly as it affects the United States border, see Kristin Heyer, *Kinship across Borders: A Christian Ethic of Immigration* (Washington, DC: Georgetown University Press, 2012). Political developments in both Europe and the United States frequently play off the global migration phenomenon, as witnessed most recently in the political campaign of Donald Trump in the United States.

[3]It therefore comes as no shock to such students that Christian theology concerns not only an understanding of the foundations of Christian faith but also their ethical heart and implication. Nor does it come as a shock to such students that the deepest challenge of the Gospel is the one that Jesus makes to the rich young man (Mk 10:17–31; Mt 19:16–30, Lk 18:18–39), nor that the paradigm for participating in the mission of Jesus is established by the Good Samaritan (Lk 10:29–37), and judgment of its authenticity established in Matthew 29.

[4]Rainer Maria Rilke, opening lines of poem, "Oh, in Childhood," in *The Unknown Rilke: Expanded Edition,* trans. Franz Wright (Oberlin, OH: Oberlin College Press, 1990), 109.

[5]See Paul Ricoeur, *The Symbolism of Evil*, trans. Emerson Buchanan (Boston: Beacon Press, 1967), 351.

[6]Jean-Luc Marion, "Metaphysics and Phenomenology: A Relief for The-

ology," in *The Visible and the Revealed,* trans. Christina M. Gschwandtner (New York: Fordham University Press, 2008), 63.

Chapter 1

[1]Charles Taylor, *A Secular Age* (Cambridge, MA: Belknap Press of Harvard University Press, 2007), 437.

[2]See ibid., 488–90. The "buffered self" is the product of a post-Durkheimian age where several factors, including the sexual revolution, have resulted in the severing of "spirituality" from religion, and religion's previous ties to a moral and civic order. A guarding of "my" spirituality against the restraints of religion results in a gradual erosion of belief in the doctrinal forms of religion. One is reminded here of Robert Bellah's "Sheilaism," a term describing a highly personalized understanding of religion as spirituality, and borrowing from various traditions. See *Habits of the Heart* (Berkeley: University of California Press, 1998). Taylor would put the 1960s and 1970s at the beginning of this post-Durkheimian reality.

[3]This is part of the process that Charles Taylor calls "disenchantment" (see below). In addition to *Secular Age,* see "Religious Mobilizations," in *Dilemmas and Connections: Selected Essays* (Cambridge, MA: Belknap Press of Harvard University Press, 2011), 148–49.

[4]More Young People Are Moving Away from Religion, But Why?" in NPR Special Series "Losing Our Religion," January 15, 2013, www.npr.org. On May 12, 2015, Pew Research Center published "America's Changing Religious Landscape" (http://www.pewforum.org), which found "that the percentage of adults (ages eighteen and older) who describe themselves as Christians has dropped by nearly eight percentage points in just seven years, from 78.4 percent in an equally massive Pew Research survey in 2007 to 70.6 percent in 2014. Over the same period, the percentage of Americans who are religiously unaffiliated—describing themselves as atheist, agnostic, or "nothing in particular"—has jumped more than six points, from 16.1 percent to 22.8 percent. The study observes: "The number of religiously unaffiliated adults has increased by roughly 19 million since 2007. There are now approximately 56 million religiously unaffiliated adults in the U.S., and this group—sometimes called religious 'nones'—is more numerous than either Catholics or mainline Protestants, according to the new survey. Indeed, the unaffiliated are now second in size only to evangelical Protestants among major religious groups in the U.S."

[5]A study published by the Pew Forum on Religion and Public Life placed "nones"—defined by Pew as those without religious affiliation or not believing in God—at 1.1 billion persons worldwide, about the same number as those who claim to be Catholic. In fact, after Christianity, at 2.2 billion, and Islam at 1.6 billion, the "nones" are the world's third largest religion. See the Pew Forum on Religion and Public Life, "The Global Religious Landscape: A Report on the Size and Distribution of the World's Major Religious Groups as of 2010," December 18, 2012, www.pewforum.org. See also Kimberly Winston, "Unbelief Is Now the World's Third-

Largest 'Religion,'" *National Catholic Reporter,* December 19, 2012, www.ncronline.org.

[6]Elizabeth A. Johnson, *Quest for the Living God* (New York: Continuum, 2005), 14.

[7]See Blaise Pascal, the *Memorial,* which reads in part:

"The year of grace 1654
Monday, November 23, day of Saint Clement, Pope and Martyr, and others in the Martyrology.
Eve of Saint Chrysogonus, Martyr and others.
From about half past ten in the evening until half past midnight.
Fire
'God of Abraham, God of Isaac, God of Jacob,' not of philosophers and scholars.
Certainty, certainty; heartfelt, joy, peace.
God of Jesus Christ.
God of Jesus Christ.
'My God and your God.'"

See *Blaise Pascal: Pensées*, trans. A. J. Krailsheimer (Harmondsworth, Eng.: Penguin Books, 1966), 309. For a penetrating analysis of the *Memorial,* see Romano Guardini, *Pascal for Our Time,* trans. Brian Thompson (New York: Herder, 1966), 33–44. Originally published in 1935 as *Christliches Bewusstsein: Versuche über Pascal.*

[8]Charles Taylor, "Western Secularity," in *Rethinking Secularism*, ed. Craig Calhoun, Mark Juergensmeyer, and Jonathan VanAntwerpen (New York: Oxford University Press, 2011), 32.

[9]For an analysis of this development, and the failure of theology to respond it, see Michael J. Buckley, *At the Origins of Modern Atheism* (New Haven, CT: Yale University Press, 1987). See in particular chapter 1, "Religion as Bankrupt: Catholic Theologians and the Origins of Modern Atheism," 37–67. Buckley also unfolds this thesis in his 1992 CTSA Presidential Address, "The Rise of Modern Atheism and the Religious Epoché," CTSA *Proceedings* 47 (1992): 69–83, http://ejournals.bc.edu.

[10]Taylor, "Western Secularity," 39. For a theological rendering of disenchantment, but seen in a more positive light as one of the effects of Christian revelation, see Ghislain Lafont, *Imagining the Catholic Church: Structured Communion in the Spirit,* trans. John J. Burkhard (Collegeville, MN: Liturgical Press, 2000), 21. In speaking of Christian antiquity, Lafont sees a "partial disenchantment" not only in religious matters, but also in philosophy and politics. "'Disenchantment' to the extent that Christian revelation freed the reality of the divine and of the human and cosmic from the realm of fable and myth; 'partial' because the return to the real does not bring about the disappearance of transcendence, spirituality, and mystery but places them in a new light." See Talal Asad's treatment of the secular, below, which locates its emergence in the Christian displacement of God from a sacred locus. One could go further and say that the Incarnation opens up the possibility of a secular realm in its own right, one that is assumed by the Divine in genuine freedom.

[11]Charles Taylor, "A Catholic Modernity?" in *Dilemmas and Connections*, 177.

[12]Jürgen Habermas, "An Awareness of What Is Missing," in *An Awareness of What Is Missing: Faith and Reason in a Post-Secular Age*, trans. Ciaran Cronin (Malden, MA: Polity Press, 2011), 16.

[13]Ibid.

[14]Talal Asad, *Formations of the Secular: Christianity, Islam, Modernity* (Stanford, CA: Stanford University Press, 2003), 25.

[15]Ibid.

[16]Ibid., 30.

[17]Available on the Vatican website: http://www.vatican.va. For a helpful discussion of this speech, see Michael Reder and Josef Schmidt, "Habermas and Religion," in *An Awareness of What Is Missing*, 8–9, and Mark Johnston, *Saving God: Religion after Idolatry* (Princeton, NJ: Princeton University Press, 2009), 70–76.

[18]Charles Taylor describes an "expressivist revolution" in the twentieth century, where an earlier linkage of religion, morality, and civic polity broke down. This left a field of "feeling" for religion that increasingly resisted mapping with church and social institutions. "Deeply felt personal insight now becomes our most precious spiritual resource." But there is little commonality among these insights: "My spiritual path has to respect those of others; it must abide by the harm principle. With this restriction, one's path can range through those which require some community to live out, even national communities or would-be state churches, but it can also range beyond to those which require only the loosest affinity groups, or just some servicing agency, like a source of advice and literature." This triumph of an ever-stronger individualist spirituality would lead to the dismantling of the power of religion to bind the parts of human life together into a coherent whole. A major factor in this development was the sexual revolution. See *Secular Age*, 486–95.

[19]I am referring here in particular to those intellectuals who are part of the academic ranks, where the development of the modern university into a system of largely unrelated departments and disciplinary silos has been accompanied by the sequestering and, in most cases, the elimination of religion or of religious studies, more so of theology, from the intellectual life of the university. For a discussion of this historical development, see George M. Mardsen and Bradley J. Longfield, *The Secularization of the Academy* (New York: Oxford University Press, 1992). In discussing those who hold that religion must decline in the face of science or its general irrelevance, Charles Taylor notes that this view "is very strong among intellectuals and academics" (*Secular Age*, 429).

[20]Cf. Bill Maher's film, *Religulous*, which mocks religion with a merciless hauteur that has abdicated serious intellectual engagement with its subject matter. For a deeper analysis that is helpful in placing this kind of phenomenon, see Bernard Schweizer, *Hating God: The Untold Story of Misotheism* (New York: Oxford University Press, 2011), which describes the phenomenon, to be distinguished from popular or "new" atheism, of

antipathy toward God, which may or may not lean toward a final atheism. Misotheists, those who hate God, "feel that humanity is the subject of divine carelessness or sadism, and they question God's love for humanity" (8).

[21]Friedrich Nietzsche, *The Gay Science*, trans. Walter Kaufmann (New York: Vintage, 1974), 181. For a masterly exegesis of this passage, see Buckley, *At the Origins of Modern Atheism*, 28–30. "Two things were poignantly obvious to Nietzsche: that the incredibility of god within the bourgeois world constitutes his death, and that this was the elimination of a god radically unimportant to those who clustered there. The god who had disappeared from conviction was finally irrelevant" (30).

[22]Jonathan Glover maintains that Nietzsche's critique extends beyond religion to include "scientific and metaphysical 'religions' as well. . . . Nietzsche wanted to preside at the funeral of *any* faith in a set of beliefs as the objective truth about things, or in external validation of anyone's way of life." See Glover, *Humanity: A Moral History of the Twentieth Century* (New Haven, CT: Yale University Press, 2000), 13.

[23]Michael J. Buckley, *Denying and Disclosing God: The Ambiguous Progress of Modern Atheism* (New Haven, CT: Yale University Press, 2004), 98. Such a view is corroborated by Glover, *Humanity*, 16: "Christian morality's rejection of the law of the jungle had almost ruined the human species: for Nietzsche, it was more than time for that morality to be overturned."

[24]In the concept of the "trace," see Gayatri Chakravorty Spivak, "Translator's Preface" to Jacques Derrida, *Of Grammatology* (Baltimore: Johns Hopkins University Press, 1974), xiii–xx. Spivak writes: "Derrida's trace is the mark of the absence of a presence, an always already absent present, of the lack at the origin that is the condition of thought and experience. For somewhat different yet similar contingencies, both Heidegger and Derrida teach us to use language in terms of a trace-structure, effacing it even as it presents its legibility" (xvii). Harkening back to Heidegger, what is true of language is also true of being, which assumes a trace structure, so that what is always already present is the absence of being. So, too, with the being of God.

[25]See, for example, John Caputo and Michael J. Scanlon, eds. *God, the Gift, and Postmodernism* (Bloomington: Indiana University Press, 1999); Gianni Vattimo, "History of Salvation, History of Interpretation," in *The Return of God: Theological Perspectives in Contemporary Philosophy*, ed. Niels Grønkjær (Odense, Denmark: Odense University Press, 1998), and *Belief*, trans. Luca D'Isanto and David Webb (Stanford, CA: Stanford University Press, 1999); Jean-Luc Marion, *God without Being*, trans. Thomas A. Carlson (Chicago: University of Chicago Press, 1991); Richard Kearney, *Anatheism: Returning to God after God* (New York: Columbia University Press, 2010). In this relatively new genre of philosophical and theological speculation, some of which has its roots in the later Heidegger, God's traces are still to be found, traces from a cultural setting in which a whole metaphysics once buttressed a world of faith in God and articulation of that faith in beliefs. These thinkers are endeavoring to establish a new way of thinking about faith and belief, one that does not presuppose the God of traditional metaphysics.

[26]Kearney, *Anatheism*, 5.

[27]For a recent expression of this thesis, see Joseph Rivera, "God and Metaphysics in Contemporary Theology: Reframing the Debate," *Theological Studies* 77 (2016): 803–22.

[28]I am limiting myself here to the Christian conception of monotheism, as enshrined in the doctrine of the Trinity, although this doctrine does depend in part on the sources of revelation also to be found in the Hebrew Scriptures. An interesting question arises when we see the conflation of Yahweh with the Christian Trinity and with the Muslim Allah. In this regard, see Mark Johnston on the dangers of theological syncretism in *Saving God*, 2–4: "A syncretistic confusion dominates modern theology because of a kind of wishful thinking, a form of thinking in which a technical theological claim (the numerical identity of the gods of the monotheisms) is the illegitimate offspring of decent and widely held desires. . . . One reason why . . . reflex syncretism is so comforting, is that taking a cold, hard look at what we do worship would leave us with the anxious questions: Do we really believe in God? Is our god really God?"

[29]Rahner held that even the denial of the existence of god keeps the word itself alive, because denial of the ineffable presupposes some sense of the ineffable. Even the denial of god is then a tacit acknowledgment of the underlying human experience of transcendence.

[30]Karl Rahner, *Foundations of Christian Faith*, trans. William Dych (New York: Crossroad, 1978), 48. One might say today that the human species would have regressed to the level of automatons. (Dych translation altered to render it in gender-inclusive language.) One might well wonder here the degree to which social media and technology are abetting what Rahner describes as a real danger. Heidegger's "Memorial Address" is apposite here on the distinction between meditative and calculative thought. See Heidegger, *Discourse on Thinking*, trans. John M. Anderson and E. Hans Freund (New York: Harper Torchbooks, 1966), 43–57.

[31]Rahner, *Foundations*, 49. It might seem to some that what Rahner imagined as something of a thought experiment has indeed come to pass, and that we are now bereft of the referent itself of the word. I would not agree at this point, although we may be moving there so that, one day, we will have arrived without knowing it, through a concrescence of losses.

[32]See Hans-Georg Gadamer, *Truth and Method,* 2nd rev. ed., trans. Joel Weinsheimer and Donald G. Marshall (New York: Crossroad, 1989), 442–53.

[33]Rahner, *Foundations*, 50.

[34]See the still splendid treatment of this passage by John Courtney Murray in *The Problem of God, Yesterday and Today* (New Haven, CT: Yale University Press, 1964), 5–15. "God first asserts the fact of his presence in the history of his people: 'I shall be there.' Second, he asserts the mystery of his own being: 'I shall be there as who I am.' His mystery is a mode of absence. Third, he asserts that, despite his absence in mystery, he will make himself known to his people: 'As who I am shall I be there'" (10). For a classic theological analysis of this passage, see Gerhard von Rad, *Old Testament Theology*, vol. 1: *The Theology of Israel's Historical Traditions*, trans. D. M. G. Stalker (New York: Harper & Row, 1962), 179–87. "It has

always been emphasized, and rightly so, that, in this passage at any rate, the [*hayah*] is to be understood in the sense of 'being present,' 'being there,' and therefore precisely not in the sense of absolute, but of relative and efficacious being—I will be there (for you)" (180).

[35]*'emet* can refer to God's fidelity (Gn 38:18ff.) where it is often linked with God's kindness (*hesed*), or the fidelity of human beings (Ps 85:12). It can also refer to a fidelity that translates as truth or what is true, as of "the true God" [*'elohe 'emet*] (1 Kgs 10:6). A hallmark of the covenant is that the fidelity is mutual between God and human beings; it is a lived relationship, where God is known in the covenantal relationship, not as an object of intellectual assent.

[36]Peter C. Phan, "Deus Migrator—God the Migrant: Migration of Theology and Theology of Migration," *Theological Studies* 77 (2016): 845–68.

[37]See Psalms 107, 116, 219, 130, and 137, as well as the entire Book of Lamentations.

[38]Bernard W. Anderson, *Understanding the Old Testament*, 2nd ed. (Englewood Cliffs, NJ: Prentice-Hall, 1966), 378.

[39]Roger Haight, *Dynamics of Theology,* 2nd ed. (Maryknoll, NY: Orbis Books, 2001), 32–48.

[40]This is a frequent image in Rahner's spiritual writings about the place of the Christian in the modern world. See Karl Rahner, "The Believer amid Unbelievers," in *Do You Believe in God?,* trans. Richard Strachan (New York: Newman Press, 1969), 19.

Chapter 2

[1]In simple language, Teresa describes the scope of the challenge of AIDS: "The work for the 'Aids' keeps growing fruitfully. No one has died without Jesus. There is so much suffering among our poor all around the world.—We are now in 77 countries over 350 houses. Can you imagine—poor people entering and leaving from all sides . . . in New York—already 50 have died a beautiful death . . .

At the beginning St. Peter would not let me enter heaven because there were no slums in heaven.—Now heaven is full of slum people. Jesus must be very happy to have those thousands coming to Him, with love from Calcutta" (*Come Be My Light: The Private Writings of the Saint of Calcutta,* ed. Brian Kolodiejchuk [New York: Doubleday, 2007], 309).

[2]Thérèse was Teresa's namesake. For a description of her own "temptations against faith" and the darkness she experienced in facing her death, see Guy Gaucher, *The Passion of Thérèse of Lisieux,* trans. Anne Marie Brennan (New York: Crossroad, 1990), 106–22. "This enduring trial that Thérèse referred to as a 'black hole,' a 'wall,' a 'tunnel,' 'fogs,' 'night,' 'darkness,' made her enter into a more marked solitude. It was indescribable and incomprehensible and made her a stranger even to her own sisters" (116).

[3]Martin Buber, "What Is Man?" in *Between Man and Man*, trans. Ronald Gregor Smith (New York: Macmillan, 1965), 127.

[4]Plato, *Timaeus* [41–47].

[5]See Augustine, *Confessions*, trans. Henry Chadwick (Oxford: Oxford University Press, 1991), and in particular book 7, ix: "In reading the Platonic books I found expressed in different words, and in a variety of ways, that the Son, 'being in the form of the Father did not think it theft to be equal with God,' because by nature he is that very thing" (p. 121). The reference is to Philippians 2:1–11, which we will consider in chapter 3. But Augustine finds the message of Scripture foreshadowed in the Platonic cosmology and metaphysics. He also refers to the aid of "the books of the Platonists" in 7.20 , (pp. 129–30). Peter Brown points out that it is in fact the works of the Neoplatonists, and in particular the *Enneads* of Plotinus, that most greatly influenced his thinking in the *Confessions*. See Peter Brown, *Augustine of Hippo* (Berkeley: University of California Press, 1967), 168: "For the Neo-Platonists provided him with the one, essential tool for any serious autobiography: they had given him a theory of the dynamics of the soul that made sense of his experiences."

[6]Buber, "What Is Man?" 128.

[7]See the first lines of Milton's *Paradise Lost,* book 1:

Of man's first disobedience, and the fruit
Of that forbidden tree, whose mortal taste
Brought death into the world, and all our woe,
With loss of Eden, till one greater man
Restore us, and regain the blissful seat,
Sing heav'nly Muse . . .

As in *The Complete Poetry and Essential Prose of John Milton*, ed. William Kerrigan, John Rumrich, and Stephen M. Fallon (New York: Modern Library, 2007), 293–94.

[8]See Walker Percy, *Lost in the Cosmos* (New York: Farrar, Straus and Giroux, 1983). This somewhat whimsical book contains, among other gems, a chapter titled "The Nowhere Self: How the Self, Which Usually Experiences Itself as Living Nowhere, Is Surprised to Find that It Lives Somewhere."

[9]The Genesis story of the Flood has progenitors in ancient Near Eastern literature. See the brief introduction to "The Epic of Gilgamesh," in *The Ancient Near East: An Anthology of Texts and Pictures*, ed. James B. Pritchard (Princeton, NJ: Princeton University Press, 2011), 39. The Genesis story is told within the framework of a theology of judgment, first introduced in the wake of the Fall. The interplay between divine justice and mercy would become a developing theme in the Jewish Scriptures, and would undergo a transformation in the teaching of Jesus, with divine justice now enveloped within and emerging from a radical understanding of divine mercy.

[10]*Cur Deus Homo* is the title of the foundational work by Saint Anselm of Canterbury. An enormously influential work for its theology of divine "satisfaction" for the sin of Adam, it is cast in the form of a dialogue between Anselm and his student, Boso. Anselm writes that human beings were made for an end "that could not be fulfilled unless God became man, and unless all things were to take place which we hold with regard to Christ." See *St. Anselm: Basic Writings*, trans. S. N. Deane (LaSalle, IL: Open Court, 1968), 177–78. For a thorough analysis of this important work, and of the polemical

context out of which it arose, see R. W. Southern, *St. Anselm: A Portrait in a Landscape* (Cambridge: Cambridge University Press, 1990), 197–227.

[11]As we know, the story concludes in the Garden of the Empty Tomb, where dislocation resulting from the catastrophe of Eden is dissolved by the encounter with a gardener whose love seems eerily familiar, and who brings Mary of Magdala back home to herself (Jn 20:11–18). The result is that she becomes an apostle, the first to announce the news of the Resurrection.

[12]"My God, my God, why have you abandoned me?" (Mt 27:46). See Karl Rahner, "Following the Crucified," *Theological Investigations* 18, trans. Edward Quinn (New York: Crossroad, 1983), 165: "In the concreteness of his death it becomes only too clear that everything fell away from him, even the perceptible security of the closeness of God's love, and in this trackless dark there prevailed silently only the mystery that in itself and in its freedom has no name and to which he nevertheless calmly surrendered himself as to eternal love and not to the hell of futility."

[13]Buber, "What Is Man?" 131.

[14]Ibid.

[15]The term "paradigm shift" comes from Thomas S. Kuhn, *The Structure of Scientific Revolutions,* 2nd ed. enl. (Chicago: University of Chicago Press, 1970).

[16]See John Hick, *Evil and the God of Love*, rev. ed. (San Francisco: HarperSanFrancisco, 1977). The book divides among three general typologies: an Augustinian type, an Irenaean type, and Hick's own proposal.

[17]See Michael Mendelson, "Saint Augustine," *Stanford Encyclopedia of Philosophy* (Winter 2012 edition), ed. Edward N. Zalta, http://plato.stanford.edu. "In both *De Libero Arbitrio* and *De Civitate Dei*, Augustine's treatment of this problem is complex and at times exceedingly obscure. . . , but his aim is clear enough. Augustine is anxious, contra the Manicheans and Cicero, to defend the compatibility of divine foreknowledge and human freedom by arguing that the free exercise of the will is among the events foreknown by God and that such foreknowledge in no way detracts from our culpability for our acts of willing [e.g. *De Libero Arbitrio* III.3 & 4; *De Civitate Dei* V.9]. The obscurity of the details notwithstanding, Augustine leaves no doubt that he wants to maintain both that God does have foreknowledge of our actions and that we are morally responsible for them."

[18]As Mendelson points out, this argument becomes progressively more pessimistic with regard to human nature, especially as the question of divine foreknowledge leads to the issue of predestination: "Thus, the human race is comprised of a *massa damnata* [*De Dono Perseverantiae* 35; see also *De Civitate Dei* 21.12], out of which God, in a manner inscrutable to us [*De Civitate Dei* 12.28], has predestined a small number to be saved [*De Civitate Dei* 21.12], and to whom he has extended a grace without which it is impossible for the will not to sin." This question of divine foreknowledge and predestination has its roots in pre-Christian thought, and was discussed by Cicero in *De Divinatione* and *De Fato*, writings known to Augustine (see Mendelson). Later, Boethius would take up these questions in his vastly influential *Consolation of Philosophy*.

[19]Augustine, *Confessions,* 1.7 (Chadwick trans., p. 9).

[20]See *Summa Theologiae* I, q. 14, a. 13. For more on this question in relation to the problem of human suffering, see Richard W. Miller, ed., *Suffering and the Christian Life* (Maryknoll, NY: Orbis Books, 2013), 83–111. Despite Thomas's refinements, Western Christianity received a view that God's foreknowledge was in some sense determinative of acts. What was the effect of this view, predestination? First, it encouraged a religiosity of aligning one's will with what one hoped was the will of God, as we were to see in the theology of John Calvin, which had an indirect effect on the shaping of Jansenism within Catholicism. Although abstracted from our day-to-day affairs, God was ultimately involved with reality on the ground, for the world had issued from his provident will. We see this view represented in the celebrated thirteenth-century image of Christ the Geometer, where Christ, with protractor in hand, measures out the dimensions of the universe.

[21]See John Thiel, *God, Evil, and Innocent Suffering: A Theological Reflection* (New York: Crossroad, 2002), esp. 39, where he concludes that Leibniz's "best of all possible worlds" theodicy "renders innocent suffering metaphysically incoherent." See also Terrence W. Tilley, *The Evils of Theodicy* (Washington, DC: Georgetown University Press, 1991), which expands the discussion beyond suffering of the innocent to the adequacy of theodicy as a way of approaching the problem of evil more broadly considered.

[22]See Herbert McCabe, *God and Evil in the Theology of St. Thomas Aquinas* (New York: Continuum, 2010): "I will show that the problem of evil arises because of the mistaken assumption that God is one among many other kinds of things—that, in fact, it is a typically metaphysical muddle due to the uncontrolled application of words outside their due contexts" (21–22). Moral evil is the result of human causality. "We are born with a nature that determines what it shall be good for us to do and what evil. But . . . there is no such context for God. God is not any kind of thing. There is nothing that it is natural for God to do, and nothing unnatural. He cannot have duties or a way of life. He has no function and no place in any order. All creatures are *his* and hence are ordered towards him. And he is not *his*. Before he does anything there is no reason for doing it rather than not doing it. There is not even a 'before.' He does not have good reasons for what he does. Rather, he *is* the reason for what he does" (127). This approach modifies the grounds for establishing a creator/creature binary: "Creatures do not *differ* from God. God is not what is left over when you remove creatures" (129).

[23]This is arguably what is going on in the "theology of the body" proposed by Pope John Paul II, which makes use of an essentialist understanding of nature and a physicalist understanding of natural law theory. For a critique of the essentialist approach to nature, see Cristina L. H. Traina, *Feminist Ethics and the Natural Law: An End to Anathemas* (Washington, DC: Georgetown University Press, 1999).

[24]Charles Taylor, *A Secular Age* (Cambridge, MA: Belknap Press of Harvard University Press, 2007), 233.

[25]Interestingly, his contemporary at Paris was John Calvin. The two apparently never met.

[26]Hugo Rahner, *Ignatius the Theologian*, trans. Michael Barry (New York: Herder, 1968).

[27]*The Spiritual Exercises of Saint Ignatius: A Translation and Commentary,* trans. George E. Ganss (Chicago: Loyola University, 1992), [236–37], 95. For an exposition of this notion of providence, see Joseph B. Wall, *The Providence of God in the Letters of St. Ignatius* [excerpt from dissertation written at the Gregorian University] (San Jose, CA: Smith-McKay, 1958), 12: "When St. Ignatius rises from a particular problem to develop at some length a generic idea of God, he develops the idea of God 'at work.' What abstract theodicy he has is a theodicy of providence. Moreover, it is the work of God in the human soul rather than the whole compass of providence that captures his attention."

[28]Although I am not proposing a process theology of God here, there are some aspects of a process theology of God that could prove helpful in developing this understanding of providence. See, for example, Joseph Bracken, "God's Will or God's Desires for Us: A Change in Worldview?" *Theological Studies* 71 (2010): 62–78. Bracken uses Whitehead to explore the implications for the language of "God's desire," an Ignatian trope, in contrast to the language of "God's will," which is typically deployed in scholastic discussions of providence.

[29]This appears in many places, and perhaps most conveniently in the *Foundations* (Karl Rahner, *Foundations of Christian Faith*, trans. William Dych [New York: Crossroad, 1978], 404): "Christianity has placed the cross on the altar, has hung it on the walls of Christian homes, and has planted it on Christian graves. Why? Evidently it is supposed to remind us that we may not be dishonest and try to suppress the hardness and darkness and death in our existence, and that . . . death is the only passage to the life which really does not die any more and which does not experience death at its innermost core."

[30]In speaking of correlating the doctrine of the Incarnation with an evolutionary view of the world, Rahner says: "The task consists, then, in showing an intrinsic affinity and the possibility of a reciprocal correlation between the two without making the Christian doctrine of incarnation a necessary and intrinsic element within the contemporary view of the world" (*Foundations*, 179). Rahner wants to preserve the Incarnation as the result of God's free prerogative, not simply a virtually inevitable moment within the evolution of the world.

[31]Rahner, *Foundations,* 404. Rahner here is turning Marx's critique of religion, as an opiate of the masses, on its head. Marx argues that this is a necessary function of religion, until religion is no longer needed.

[32]Karl Rahner, "Why Does God Allow Us to Suffer?" *Theological Investigations* 19, trans. Edward Quinn (New York: Crossroad, 1983), 206.

[33]See McCabe, *God and Evil*, 105: "Nothing whatever about the world follows from any statement about what God is in himself."

[34]Karl Rahner, *The Eternal Year,* trans. John Shea (Baltimore: Helicon Press, 1964), 65–72.

[35]Augustine, *Confessions*, 3.6 (Chadwick trans., p. 43).

[36]See Edward Schillebeeckx: "But the God of Christians is 'not a God of the dead, but a God of the living' (Matt. 22:32). In other words, *this* concept of God ascribes to him only and solely positivity: 'God is love' (1 John 4:10, 16), who is according to his being a promoter of the good and an opponent of everything evil. And then for the believer who wishes to follow after God the *orientation* for all activity can only lie in the promotion of the good and in the resistance to evil, injustice and suffering in all its forms." See *The Schillebeeckx Reader*, ed. and trans. Robert J. Schreiter (New York: Crossroad, 1987), 266; originally published as "Glaube und Moral," in *Ethik im Kontext des Glaubens* (Fribourg/Freiburg i. Br.: Universitätsverlag, 1978), 17–45.

[37]McCabe, *God and Evil*, 128.

Chapter 3

[1]See "Meditation on the Two Standards: of Christ and of Lucifer," in *The Spiritual Exercises of Saint Ignatius*, trans. George E. Ganss (Chicago: Loyola University Press, 1992), [136–48], 65–67.

[2]Hugo Rahner, *Ignatius the Theologian*, trans. Michael Barry (New York: Herder and Herder, 1968), 12. See also my "Between Earth and Heaven: Ignatian Imagination and the Aesthetics of Liberation," in *Through a Glass Darkly: Essays in the Religious Imagination*, ed. John C. Hawley (New York: Fordham University Press, 1966), 50–69.

[3]H. Rahner, *Ignatius the Theologian*, 9.

[4]*Spiritual Excercises* [102], Ganss trans., 56. This image, constructed by Ignatius, is unintentionally echoed in Ingmar Bergman's 1975 film rendering of Mozart's opera, *The Magic Flute*, where putti look down on the action below through what seem to be cardboard cutout clouds, evoking a benign heavenly gaze upon human weakness and folly.

[5]*Spiritual Excercises* [108], Ganss trans., 57.

[6]*Spiritual Excercises* [109], Ganss trans., 58. We find here an indication of the importance of a sense of time and history in Ignatius's spirituality, and in the exercise of Ignatian imagination. The distance of the event of the Incarnation from the present moment is reduced by considering it to have occurred but lately, *nuevamente*. Here the imagination does more than reconstruct a past event; it collapses the present and the past into God's eternality.

[7]H. Rahner, *Ignatius the Theologian*, 17. Translation slightly emended.

[8]Johannes Baptist Metz, *Poverty of Spirit*, trans. John Drury, rev. ed. by Carole Farris (New York: Paulist Press, 1968, 1998).

[9]I am indebted to John Murphy, SJ, for pointing out that the Greek root for humiliation used here in Philippians (*tapein*) also occurs in the Magnificat (Lk 1:48), which refers to the humble state of Mary, the Mother of God.

[10]See my "*Instrumentum Divinitatis* in Thomas Aquinas: Recovering the Divinity of Christ," *Theological Studies* 52 (1991): 451–75.

[11]Leo I, "Letter to Flavian of Constantinople," 13 June 449, as in *The Christian Faith in the Doctrinal Documents of the Catholic Church*, ed. Jacques Dupuis (New York: Alba House, 2001), 226.

[12]"Symbol of Chalcedon (451), in *Christian Faith in the Doctrinal Documents*, ed. Dupuis, 227.

[13]Leo I, "First Christmas Sermon," as in *Christ and His Mission: Christology and Soteriology*, ed. James M. Carmody and Thomas E. Clarke (Westminster, MD: Newman Press, 1966), 119.

[14]Here the pope is rejecting any notions of a monophysitism that would reduce the full and authentic human nature of the incarnate Son, and thus render the Incarnation a myth, leaving God in the heavens, remote from human affairs. Monophysitism was rejected by the Council of Chalcedon (451). He is also rejecting monotheletism, which would have ascribed only a divine will and intentionality to Jesus. This view was rejected by the Third Council of Constantinople (681).

[15]John Paul II, "Redemptor Hominis" 8, http://w2.vatican.va. Translation slightly altered.

[16]Rahner suggests that the human was created by God in order that God might become incarnate: "When God wants to be what is not God, man comes to be . . . [I]n this way he becomes precisely someone who participates in the infinite mystery of God, just as a question participates in its answer, and just as the question is borne only by the possibility of the answer itself." Karl Rahner, *Foundations of Christian Faith*, trans. William Dych (New York: Crossroad, 1978), 225.

[17]Metz, *Poverty of Spirit*, 12.

[18]Kathryn Tanner, *Jesus, Humanity, and the Trinity: A Brief Systematic Theology* (Minneapolis: Fortress Press, 2001), 3–4. As Rahner would put it, human dependence and autonomy grow in direct, not inverse proportion: "Because in the Incarnation the Logos creates the human reality by assuming it, and assumes it by emptying *himself*, for this reason there also applies here, and indeed in the most radical and specific and unique way, the axiom for understanding every relationship between God and creatures, namely, that closeness and distance, or being at God's disposal and being autonomous, do not vary for creatures in inverse, but rather in direct proportion" (*Foundations*, 226).

[19]Metz, *Poverty of Spirit*, 33–34.

[20]James F. Keenan, *The Works of Mercy: The Heart of Catholicism*, 2nd ed. (Lanham, MD: Rowman & Littlefield, 2008), 145.

Chapter 4

[1]Ignatius, "Contemplation to Attain Love," in *The Spiritual Exercise Exercises of Saint Ignatius,* trans. George E. Ganss (Chicago: Loyola University Press, 1992), [136–48], 94.

[2]But in Ignatian spirituality there is no inherent opposition between the habits of contemplation and activity in the world. The aim of one steeped in this tradition is to become a *contemplativus in actione*—entering into activity while imbued with a contemplative spirit and foundation. The phrase is attributed to Geronimo Nadal, but its provenance and Nadal's own understanding of the relation between the contemplative and the active are more complicated than commonly presumed by many Jesuit commentators.

See Philip Endean, *Karl Rahner and Ignatian Spirituality* (Oxford: Oxford University Press, 2001), 74.

[3]Emily Dickinson, as quoted by Richard B. Sewall, *The Life of Emily Dickinson*, 2 vols. (New York: Farrar, Straus and Giroux, 1974), 2:462.

[4]The term "the crucified people" has its provenance in the work of fellow Jesuit philosopher-theologian, Ignacio Ellacuría. See my essay "Theology in the Light of Human Suffering: A Note on 'Taking the Crucified Down from the Cross,'" in *Hope and Solidarity: Jon Sobrino's Challenge to Christian Theology*, ed. Stephen J. Pope (Maryknoll, NY: Orbis Books, 2008), 16–30, esp. 18–20. For a more thorough presentation of the motif, see Robert Lassalle-Klein, *Blood and Ink: Ignacio Ellacuría, Jon Sobrino, and the Jesuit Martyrs of the University of Central America* (Maryknoll, NY: Orbis Books, 2014), 308–13. Lassalle-Klein traces Ellacuría's coinage to the historical realism of Spanish philosopher Xavier Zubiri. The "crucified people" of El Salvador could stand as a proxy for the crucified peoples who are in literal dislocation throughout the world today.

[5]Jon Sobrino, *Jesus the Liberator: A Historical Theological View*, trans. Paul Burns and Francis McDonagh (Maryknoll, NY: Orbis Books, 1993), 254–55.

[6]Ibid., 256. There follow here in the remaining pages of this remarkable book what may be some of the most trenchant yet lyrical passages ever written in the annals of liberation theology.

[7]See Jon Sobrino, *Where Is God? Earthquake, Terrorism, Barbarity, and Hope*, trans. Margaret Wilde (Maryknoll, NY: Orbis Books, 2004).

[8]Similarly, the European theologian Clemens Sedmak has been a pioneer in the development of a whole theological movement, transformation theology, the heart of which is that the disruptions of history are sites for the raw revelation of God, beyond the confines of sanctioned theologies, and are also calls to transformation of our way of being in the world. See Oliver Davies, Clemens Sedmak, and Paul D. Janz, *Transformation Theology: Church in the World* (London: T&T Clark, 2007).

[9]At the outset it should be said that Sobrino's contribution to a theology of suffering is not so much a theology *about* suffering as it is a theology written *from* and *within* suffering, the contexts of suffering that have shaped his life and career in El Salvador for the past several decades. The suffering that motivates his theology is not hidden: it is the suffering that comes upon the impoverished and politically vulnerable by powers beyond themselves, pressing down on them with the force of an affliction. It is, furthermore, the suffering of injustice that compounds even the ordinary sufferings of life. This reference to "affliction" is from Simone Weil (*malheur*). See Weil, "The Love of God and Affliction," in *Waiting for God*, trans. Emma Craufurd (New York: Harper & Row, 1951), 67–82. For an explanation of the term, see my *Unwanted Wisdom: Suffering, the Cross, and Hope* (New York: Continuum, 2005), 35–37.

[10]César A. Chelala, "Central America's Health Plight," *Christian Science Monitor*, March 22, 1990. See http://www.csmonitor.com.

[11]"To Have Courage and Prophetic Audacity: Dialogue of Pope Francis

with the Jesuits Gathered in the 36th General Congregation," October 24, 2016, http://www.laciviltacattolica.it.

[12]See *Laudato Si'*, 25, http://w2.vatican.va.

[13]This trope of "taking the crucified down from their crosses" might seem counterintuitive to the Christian imagination in the sense (a) that it was in fact the Cross of Christ that guaranteed our salvation and that salvation was not achieved by any interruption in the crucifixion of Jesus; and (b) that there is a strong spiritual pedigree in Christianity to identify with Christ crucified, to be placed with the Son suffering on the Cross. Sobrino's trope does nothing to deny the truth of the Cross of Christ, not even the desire to be placed with the suffering Son. But he is implicitly critiquing a spirituality of the Cross that stands passively in the face of suffering, and that assigns whole peoples to suffering under the sign of the Cross. Jesus's saving death on the cross was saving precisely in that it brought to an end the "logic" of the Cross and its use as a justification for suffering. In the present dispensation, therefore, crucifixion is indeed to be interrupted, in the name of the Cross, even as the disciple of Jesus may well identify with his sufferings on the Cross, not for suffering's sake, but "for our sake and for the sake of our salvation."

[14]The "dangerous memory" or "*memoria passionis*" of the crucified is derived from a key motif of Johannes Metz, who summarizes it succinctly in his essay, "On the Way to a Postidealist Theology," in *A Passion for God: The Mystical-Political Dimension of Christianity*, trans. J. Matthew Ashley (New York: Paulist Press, 1998), 47–53. This sentiment is reflected in Sobrino's own work. He argues that we risk losing the scandal of the cross if we forget that its meaning is revealed within "the real crucified world" of martyrs. He has in mind not only Archbishop Romero, who was assassinated as a consequence of his own acceptance of the call to discipleship, but all those who lost their lives in El Salvador during the civil war because of their witness to faith. See Sobrino, "The Spirituality of Persecution and Martyrdom," in *Spirituality of Liberation* (Maryknoll, NY: Orbis, 1989), 87–88, where Sobrino provides a list of the martyrs and includes, beyond that list, "Many other pastoral ministers and lay missionaries, delegates and ministers of the Word, catechists and sacristans, Caritas workers and human rights groups; many Protestant brothers and sisters, pastors and ministers, deacons and preachers; countless campesinos and Amerindians, workers and students, teachers and journalists, nurses, doctors, and intellectuals; persecuted and murdered for the reign of God." "Woe to human beings and believers if they forget the crucifixion!" Sobrino, *Jesus the Liberator*, 235.

[15]See Karl Rahner, *Foundations of Christian Faith*, trans. William Dych (New York: Crossroad, 1978), 404.

[16]See Jon Sobrino, *The Principle of Mercy: Taking the Crucified People from the Cross* (Maryknoll, NY: Orbis Books, 1994), 49–57.

[17]Ibid., 56. These two parts of Sobrino's approach to the crucified peoples—taking them down from the cross and seeing in them the source of salvation—are in fact a reflection of the deeper structure of his theology of suffering established in the life and ministry of Jesus. We find these themes expressed very early on in his 1982 Christology, *Jesus in Latin*

America, trans. Robert R. Barr (Maryknoll, NY: Orbis Books, 1987). Here we find the familiar motifs of the crucified people and of their embodiment in history as the Suffering Servant. However, rather than focus on taking them down from the crosses of suffering, Sobrino here focuses on how the crucified people follow as disciples in the pattern of Jesus and thus offer the larger church an example to follow. They enact Jesus's message by virtue of who they are, unmasking the false political and economic gods that oppress them (162–63). At this stage, then, the suffering of the crucified peoples is salvific to the degree that it is an entrée into a lived discipleship of Jesus that includes the enactment of the saving, liberating work of Jesus. And this becomes a model for understanding the church as a community of disciples in solidarity with the suffering.

[18]Sobrino, *Principle of Mercy*, 53.

[19]Ibid., 55–56.

[20]Ibid., 56.

[21]Sobrino, *Jesus in Latin America*, 163.

[22]Sobrino, *Jesus the Liberator*, 238.

[23]Ibid., 240.

[24]Ibid., 244.

[25]Ibid., 246.

[26]For a balanced and sympathetic critique of the suffering of God implied in Sobrino's theology, see Eugene R. Schlesinger, "The Church's Eucharistic Poverty in the Theologies of Jon Sobrino and Hans Urs von Balthasar," *Theological Studies* 77 (2016): 627–51.

[27]Jon Sobrino, *Christ the Liberator: A View from the Victims,* trans. Paul Burns (Maryknoll, NY: Orbis Books, 2001).

[28]Ibid., 4–5. Sobrino was a witness to that of which he speaks, in the form of massacres of innocent poor people, e.g., at El Mozote—a form of violence that has been replicated numerous times around the world since the civil war in El Salvador came to an end. Consider Rwanda, Bosnia, and Darfur, and now the killing fields of Syria and Iraq as well as of Nigeria and other places.

[29]Ibid., 37 ("Yahweh" in the original).

[30]Ibid., 39.

[31]Ibid., 44.

[32]Ibid., 45.

[33]Ibid., 47.

[34]Ibid., 49.

[35]Ibid., 48.

Chapter 5

[1]Gerhard Lohfink, *Jesus of Nazareth: What He Wanted, Who He Was*, trans. Linda M. Maloney (Collegeville, MN: Liturgical Press, 2013).

[2]Ibid., 73.

[3]Ibid., 99.

[4]For a nuanced report of Bonhoeffer's participation, and of his insistence on what he considered to be he ethical demands of the Sermon on the Mount (Mt 5–7), see Eberhard Bethge, *Dietrich Bonhoeffer: Theologian,*

Christian, Man for His Times: A Biography, rev. ed., ed. Victoria J. Barnett, trans. Eric Mosbacher (Minneapolis: Fortress Press, 2000), 366–72.

[5]Dietrich Bonhoeffer, *Life Together,* trans. John W. Doberstein (New York: Harper & Row, 1954).

[6]Dietrich Bonhoeffer, *Letters and Papers from Prison,* greatly enlarged edition, trans. Reginald Fuller, Frank Clark, et al.; ed. Eberhard Bethge (New York: Macmillan, 1971). Hereafter abbreviated as *LPP*.

[7]Letter of 30 April 1944 to Eberhard Bethge, *LPP*, 279–81.

[8]Ibid.

[9]Letter of 8 June 1944 to Bethge, *LPP*, 325–26.

[10]See Dietrich Bonhoeffer, *The Cost of Discipleship*, trans. Reginald Fuller and Irmgard Booth (New York: Macmillan, 1949). Here Bonhoeffer contrasts "cheap grace," a view of God that leads to a way of describing the kind of Christianity that demands nothing, and "costly grace," a view of God's acting toward us that demands a very high ethical standard. For a presentation of the various ways Bonhoeffer presented this concept of "religionless Christianity," see Bethge, *Dietrich Bonhoeffer*, 863–80. The discussion by Eric Metaxas in his *Bonhoeffer: Pastor, Martyr, Prophet, Spy* (Nashville, TN: Thomas Nelson, 2010), 465–69, lacks the subtlety of Bethge's presentation. André Dumas's analysis of Bonhoeffer's understanding of religion still stands as the best treatment of this topic. See Dumas, *Dietrich Bonhoeffer: Theologian of Reality*, trans. Robert McAfee Brown (New York: Macmillan, 1968), 163–214.

[11]Like Bonhoeffer, Delp wrote from his prison cell, a collection published as *The Prison Meditations of Father Delp*, introduction by Thomas Merton (New York: Herder and Herder, 1963), reprinted as *Alfred Delp, SJ: Prison Writings* (Maryknoll, NY: Orbis Books, 2004).

[12]Karl Rahner, *On Prayer* (Collegeville, MN: Liturgical Press, 1993), 11. This book was originally published in 1967. Translation slightly emended to reflect US spelling conventions.

[13]Karl Rahner, *Foundations of Christian Faith*, trans. William Dych (New York: Crossroad, 1978), 129–33.

[14]For an extended discussion of the various meanings of the term "anonymous Christian" used by Rahner, see my "Introduction: Improbable Encounters?" in *Rahner beyond Rahner: A Great Theologian Encounters the Pacific Rim* (Lanham, MD: Rowan and Littlefield/Sheed and Ward, 2005), xiii–xviii. For an excellent critique of the concept, see Jeanine Hill Fletcher, "Rahner and Religious Diversity," in *The Cambridge Companion to Karl Rahner*, ed. Declan Marmion and Mary E. Hines (Cambridge: Cambridge University Press, 2005), 235–48.

[15]See Karl Rahner, "A 'Wintry' Church and the Opportunities for Christianity," in *Faith in a Wintry Season: Conversations and Interviews with Karl Rahner in the Last Years of His Life*, ed. P. Imhof and H. Biallowons, trans. H. Egan (New York: Crossroad, 1991), 189–200.

[16]See Paul Tillich, "You Are Accepted," in *The Shaking of the Foundations* (New York: Charles Scribner's Sons, 1948), 153–63.

[17]Rahner, Foundations of Christian Faith, 406.

[18]For an excellent summary of these topics, see Joshua M. Moritz,

"Evolutionary Biology and Theological Anthropology," in *The Routledge Companion to Theological Anthropology*, ed. Joshua R. Farris and Charles Taliaferro (New York: Routledge, 2016), 45–56.

[19]For a discussion of some of these thinkers, see my "Mystagogy and Mission: The Challenge of Nonbelief and the Task of Theology," *Theological Studies* 76 (2015): 7–28.

[20]This echoes Rahner's theology of grace; see *Foundations of Christian Faith*, 120.

[21]Tanner is quoting Dionysius the Areopagite. See Kathryn Tanner, *Jesus, Humanity, and the Trinity: A Brief Systematic Theology* (Minneapolis: Fortress Press, 2001), 1.

[22]Ibid., 80.

[23]Ibid., 81.

[24]Ibid.

[25]This phrase is borrowed from the title of the book by Leszek Kolakowski, *God Owes Us Nothing: A Brief Remark on Pascal's Religion and on the Spirit of Jansenism* (Chicago: University of Chicago Press, 1995). The point is made by Herbert McCabe in *God and Evil in the Theology of St. Thomas Aquinas* (New York: Continuum, 2010), 127. See Chapter 2, n.22.

[26]*The Spiritual Exercise Exercises of Saint Ignatius,* trans. George E. Ganss (Chicago: Loyola University Press, 1992), [231], 94.

[27]Lucia Cerna and Mary Jo Ignoffo, *La Verdad: A Witness to the Salvadoran Martyrs* (Maryknoll, NY: Orbis Books, 2014), 146.

[28]Notes from a public interview with Lucia Cerna at Santa Clara University, November 12, 2014.

Epilogue

[1]This distinction has an ancient provenance, expressed variously by medieval theologians, notably Thomas Aquinas, especially in his treatise on faith in the *Summa Theologiae* 2–2, qq. 1–7. For a careful discussion of the distinction and deeper discussion of "faith" in Catholic theology, Juan Alfaro comments: "Theologians, recognizing the complexity and intrinsic unity of the act of faith, distinguish in it the following basic dimensions: faith as knowledge of revealed truth (believing in God who reveals himself in Christ: '*fides quae creditur*'); faith as trusting obedience to God and as a personal encounter with him: '*fides qua creditur*' (believing God, the formal structure of faith" ("Faith," in *Encyclopedia of Theology: The Concise* Sacramentum Mundi, ed. Karl Rahner (New York: Seabury, 1975), 500); see also Karl Rahner, "Faith between Rationality and Emotion," in *Theological Investigations* 16, trans. David Morland (London: Darton, Longman and Todd, 1979), 73, where he identifies *fides quae* with "faith as object" and *fides qua* with "faith as personal act."

[2]See Alfaro, "Faith," and Rahner, "What Is a Dogmatic Statement?" in *Theological Investigations* 5, trans. Karl-H. Kruger (Baltimore: Helicon, 1966), 48: "A dogmatic statement is a statement of faith . . . not only in as far as it is *fides quae creditur* but also in as far as it is *fides qua creditur.*" See also Rahner, "The Faith of the Christian Church and the Doctrine of the Church,"

in *Theological Investigations* 14, trans. David Bourke (New York: Seabury, 1976), 39: "*Fides quae* and *fides qua* [the content of faith and the process of the act of faith] are identical in their origins because the fundamental reality which is believed in, the self-communication of God to the human person, namely the Holy Spirit, is also the principle of faith itself, its sustaining force, and its active movement." There is an entire phenomenology of faith presumed here, one that situates the act of faith in transcendental freedom and understands faith to be the realization of that freedom. Cf. Rahner, "Faith between Rationality and Emotion," 64–66. Geoffrey D. Dunn observes: "As many a modern fundamental theologian would point out, the separation of *fides quae* from *fides qua* is not always possible. What one believes and how one acts are intricately interwoven." Dunn, "Heresy and Schism according to Cyprian of Carthage," *Journal of Theological Studies* 55 (2004): 551.

[3]I am taking this notion of "beliefs" from Roger Haight, *Dynamics of Theology*, 2nd ed. (Maryknoll, NY: Orbis Books, 2001), 33 (and passim), where he argues that faith is understood as an individual act with regard to revealed truth that has an inner dynamism toward communication. Because it cannot rest as a private matter, faith expresses itself in "beliefs." Haight maintains a constant creative and interpretive tension between the act of faith and its self-expression in beliefs, but also a clear distinction between them. What faith and beliefs have in common is a focus on what is of "ultimate concern" (Paul Tillich).

[4]George Lindbeck raises this propositionalist approach as one possibility; see his *The Nature of Doctrine: Religion and Theology in a Post-Liberal Age* (Louisville, KY: Westminster John Knox Press, 1984). His own position, the cultural-linguistic approach, is not strictly speaking propositionalist, but takes into account the effects of cultural variations on the formulations of doctrine, which nevertheless have a formal priority over experience. In a broad sense, then, the *fides quae* comes before the *fides qua*, at least in the order of our understanding of the ongoing life of faith.

[5]See Christian Wiman, *My Bright Abyss: Meditation of a Modern Believer* (New York: Farrar, Straus & Giroux, 2013), who seems to establish a sharp distinction between faith as a kind of ephemeral experience of movement toward God, and belief as propositional, pertaining to a fixed world of objective givens: "Faith steals upon you like dew; some days you wake and it is there. And like dew, it gets burned off in the rising sun of anxieties, ambitions, distractions" (93). "Faith is nothing more—but how much this is—than a motion of the soul toward God. It is not belief. Belief has objects—Christ was resurrected, God created the earth—faith does not" (139). Wiman does not propose these terms as a systematic theologian, but as a poet.

[6]Karl Rahner, "Possible Courses for the Theology of the Future," in *Theological Investigations* 13, trans. David Bourke (New York: Crossroad, 1983), 32–60. Elsewhere Rahner writes: "It is not only the '*fides quae*' that must come to terms with God as mystery, but also the '*fides qua*'. The act of faith as such in itself, and not merely its conceptual objectifications, must in some sense come to terms with the mystery as such. For this too theology . . . should constitute a 'mystagogia' leading people to the experience of grace, and should not merely speak of grace as of a material subject which

is present in a person's life solely through the conceptions which one formulates of it." See Rahner, "Reflections on Methodology in Theology," in *Theological Investigations* 11, trans. David Bourke (New York: Crossroad, 1983), 110–11. See also Rahner, "The Teaching Office of the Church in the Present-Day Crisis of Authority," in *Theological Investigations* 12, trans. David Bourke (New York: Crossroad, 1982), 23; and Rahner, "Faith between Rationality and Emotion," esp. 72–73.

[7]Ibid., 41.

[8]See Antonius Brekelmans, "Professions de foi dans l'eglise primitive: Origine et fonction," *Concilium* 51, no. 1 (1970): 30. See also Joseph Ratzinger, *Introduction to Christianity*, trans. J. R. Foster (New York: Seabury, 1979), 50–64.

[9]Michael C. McCarthy, "Modalities of Belief in Ancient Christian Debate," *Journal of Early Christian Studies* 17, no. 4 (2000): 605–34.

[10]Ibid., 608.

[11]One major early exception is the work of Robert Gregg and Dennis Groh, *Early Arianism: A View of Salvation* (Philadelphia: Fortress Press, 1981), which situates the controversy within the patterns of popular religion and understandings of salvation.

[12]See Catherine Bell, *Ritual Theory/Ritual Practice* (New York: Oxford University Press, 1992).

[13]These include "Belief: A Classificatory Lacuna and Disciplinary 'Problem,'" "Belief, Beliefs, Believing: Declensions of 'The Problem,'" and an untitled talk given at the Institute of Buddhist Studies, Graduate Theological Union, Berkeley, on October 5, 2006 (Buddhist Institute talk). These are all housed in the Catherine Bell Research Materials and Writings Collection, Santa Clara University.

[14]Bell, Buddhist Institute talk, 22.

[15]Ibid., 27.

[16]Ibid.

[17]Ibid., 28–29.

[18]The Catholic reader will wish to take note of the notion of the "hierarchy of truths" first enunciated by the Second Vatican Council in *Unitatis Redintegratio*, ¶11: "When comparing doctrines with one another, they [theologians] should remember that in Catholic doctrine there exists a 'hierarchy' of truths, since they vary in their relation to the fundamental Christian faith." This has been subject to considerable and controversial development by the Roman magisterium since the closing of the council. The fundamental idea, however, antedates the council, in the venerable and highly useful notion of "theological notes," whereby various types of teaching can be distinguished in terms of their proximity to divine revelation. For example, the pope's allocution at a Wednesday audience does not have the same weight as a conciliar teaching. For a helpful essay on this topic, see Harold E. Ernst, "The Theological Notes and the Interpretation of Doctrine," *Theological Studies* 63 (2002):813–25.

[19]Talal Asad, *Formations of the Secular: Christianity, Islam, Modernity* (Stanford, CA: Stanford University Press, 2003), 25.

Index

Anselm of Canterbury, 41, 51, 85
anthropodicy, 64, 67
Aquinas, Thomas, 44, 46
Asad, Talal, 25, 93
atheism, 23, 33
  God of modern theism, rejecting, 22
  New Atheists, 27
  post-atheistic sense of loss, 29–30
  temptation of atheism, 39, 42
  Augustine, Saint, 40, 43–44, 49, 91

Babylonian exile, 34–35
Barth, Karl, 5, 77, 84
Bell, Catherine, 92–93
Benedict XVI, Pope, 26–27
Bonhoeffer, Dietrich, 76, 77–80, 82
Buber, Martin, 3, 39, 40, 42
Buckley, Michael, 29
Catholic frustration with magisterium, 11–12

Cerna, Lucia, 74–75, 87
climate change and suffering of the poor, 65
Confessing Church, 77–78
Council of Chalcedon, 56–57
Council of Nicaea, 56
the crucified peoples, 63–65, 66–68, 72, 73, 90

Deism, 46
Delp, Alfred, 80
discipleship
  costliness of discipleship, 79
  distributing the goods of God, 86
  fides quae and *fides qua creditur*, realizing in discipleship, 89
  Finkenwalde seminary as a model for discipleship, 77
  living the teachings of Jesus, 75–76
  martyrdom, discipleship unto, 80
  as a mystagogy of believing, 95
  self-transcendence of, 94
disenchantment process, 23, 46
dislocation
  divine dislocation
    dislocation of God, 1, 4, 15, 16, 21, 41, 75, 93
    incarnation of the Son leading to, 51, 61
    kenosis and, 15, 58, 60, 84
    in Letter to the Philippians, 54–55
  existential dislocation, 2–4, 14, 36, 42, 82, 90
  martyrdom as the ultimate dislocation, 80
  ontological dislocation, 2, 3, 4, 23, 60, 90
  poverty as root cause of dislocation, 8
  of refugees and migrants, 14–15, 62
  of sinfulness, 59
  solidarity with the dislocated, 4, 15, 76, 87
  spiritual dislocation, 3, 12, 15, 42
docetism, 56

ecclesiasticism, 12, 13
El Salvador, 63–64, 67, 74
Ellacuría, Ignacio, 66, 72, 73
evil, 2, 43, 48, 49, 50, 51, 78

Francis, Pope, 5, 62, 64, 65
Francis, Saint, 60
free will, 43–44

Gadamer, Hans-Georg, 32
God
  Abraham, God of, 3, 22, 35, 36
  in Aristotelian cosmos, 39–40
  divine foreknowledge, 43–44, 47
  forgotten God, 30–33, 36, 81
  incomprehensibility of God, 48
  Moses, God of, 33–34, 37, 80, 87
  silence of God, 68–69, 70–71
  solidarity of God with humanity, 55, 60, 69
  theism, God of
    death of God, 28–29
    in debates between religion and science, 49
    describing, 21–22
    human experience, not correlating with, 79
    liberal secularist myth as rival to, 25
    Providential Deism and, 46
    rejection of beliefs about, 36
    suffering and, 40–41

Habermas, Jürgen, 23–24
Haight, Roger, 6, 36
Harnack, Adolf von, 26
Hick, John, 43
homelessness
  epoch of homelessness, 3, 39, 40, 42, 44, 49
  homeless faith of contemporary Christians, 37
  homelessness of humanity, 15, 59
  literal homelessness of Jesus, 41
  remoteness of God and, 4
  worldwide sense of, 8, 14
homoousios concept, 56, 57

Ignatius of Loyola, 48, 50, 62
  contemplation on the incarnation, 60
  divine *kenosis,* imagining, 52–54
  expression of love in deeds, 61, 63
  Spiritual Exercises of Saint Ignatius, 47, 52, 61, 87
  theology of, 46–47

Jacob, 13, 30
John Paul II, Pope, 5, 57–58, 83
John XXIII, Pope, 5, 83
Johnson, Elizabeth, 6, 21–22, 25, 36, 40

Kearney, Richard, 30
Keenan, James, 59
kenosis
  church councils, influence on *kenosis* concept, 56
  as divine dislocation, 15, 58
  Ignatius on *kenosis* saving souls from hell, 52–53
  kenosis of God in Jesus, 60, 84
  strength of God in *kenosis,* 86
  of the suffering believer, 49
Kushner, Tony, 19

Lampedusa, 7, 62
Leibniz, Gottfried, 43
Leo I, Pope, 56, 57
Lohfink, Gerhard, 75
"Losing Our Religion" (radio series), 21

magisterium, 11–12
Marion, Jean-Luc, 17, 84
martyrdom, 16, 76, 78, 80
McCarthy, Michael, 91–92
Metz, Johannes, 54, 56, 58, 67, 83
migrants and refugees, 3, 6–7, 62, 65
monophysitism, 56
Moses, 19, 26, 37
  covenant with the Lord, 35
  encounter with nameless Deity, 13–14, 33–34
  God of Moses, 80, 87
Mother Teresa of Calcutta, 38–39, 42
mystagogy, 17, 91
  baptism, belief beginning with, 94
  defining, 13
  discipleship and, 95
  expression of faith through practices, 93

Rahner, referencing, 60
as the theology of the future, 90

natural law, 26, 45
Nietzsche, Friedrich, 14, 28, 29
"nones" as religiously unaffiliated, 20

Pascal, Blaise, 36, 42, 50
Paul VI, Pope, 83
Phan, Peter, 34
poverty, 15, 59
of Christ, reflected in Saint Francis, 60
of the crucified peoples, 63, 66
the poor as instruments of salvation, 68
suffering of the poor, 64, 65, 67
victimization of the poor, 70
Poverty of Spirit (Metz), 56, 58

Rahner, Hugo, 46, 52, 53
Rahner, Karl, 10, 83, 87
on Christian diaspora, 37, 76, 82
forgotten God scenario, 30–33, 36, 81
God as far and near to us, 49
grace as all, 86
Ignatius of Loyola, historical scholarship on, 46
on the incarnation, 51
Kathryn Tanner as influenced by, 84, 85
mystagogy of faith, 60, 90
on suffering, 42, 47–48
World War II, affected by, 80–81
Resurrection praxis, 16, 72–73
Ricoeur, Paul, 12
Rilke, Rainer Maria, 1, 10
Romero, Oscar, 16, 61, 67

scientism, 24
Scotus, Duns, 85
secularism, 33, 90
Bonhoeffer, questioning the secular, 79
Christians as silent witnesses in a secularized environment, 82
postsecular era, 24
secularity thesis, 22–23, 25
secularization as a wedge between faith and reason, 27
sin, 53, 59, 72
Adam, sin of, 41
Anselm on human sinfulness, 85
Augustine on suffering and sin, 43–44
confession of sin in Confessing Church tradition, 77
history of sin, 2, 60
Jesus as exempt from, 57, 58
power of sin, 52
sins of injustice, 64
the suffering poor and, 68
Sobrino, Jon
conversion of Christian vocation, calling for, 67
on the crucified peoples, 62–63, 66, 68, 72
praxis of Resurrection, 16
silence of God, 68–69, 70–71
suffering of the poor, 64
on victims of history, 69–70, 72
solidarity, 9, 62, 67
with the crucified peoples, 16, 63, 68, 90
discipleship, leading to, 75, 76
with the dislocated, 4, 15, 87
of God with humanity, 55, 60, 69
"spiritual but not religious" category, 20, 79
suffering, 42, 60, 68
Augustine on suffering and sin, 43–44
autonomy of nature, suffering due to, 45
belief as difficult with presence of suffering, 1, 38–39
of the cosmos, God acting upon, 49
of the crucified peoples, 63–65, 66, 73
divine dislocation into suffering, 55
God of Moses, found in the suffering of the Hebrews, 15
history of sin, suffering resulting from, 2
as inescapable, 47–48
Jacob and the suffering of dislocation, 13
liberation of the suffering poor, 67

Mother Teresa as witness to suffering, 38–39
physical suffering and God of theism, 40–41
the poor, disproportionate suffering of, 64, 65
silence of the suffering God, 69
solidarity with sufferers, 3, 4, 15, 16, 62
of the victims of history, 70, 71
Summa Theologiae (Aquinas), 44

Tanner, Kathryn, 59, 76, 84–86
Taylor, Charles, 20, 22, 23, 45–46
theodicy, 43–46, 49, 67, 68
Thiel, John, 44
Tilley, Terrence, 44

Vatican I, 11
Vatican II, 57–58, 82–83
victims of history, 69–70, 72